GRADUATE STUDY IN PSYCHOLOGY
Your Guide to Success

ABOUT THE AUTHOR

Tara L. Kuther, Ph.D. is Associate Professor of psychology at Western Connecticut State University, where she teaches courses in child, adolescent, and adult development. She values opportunities to conduct collaborative research with students and is active in the Council for Undergraduate Research (CUR) as Psychology Counselor, and CUR representative to the Society for Teaching of Psychology, Division 2 of the American Psychological Association. Dr. Kuther is Chair of the Instructional Resource Award Task Force of the Office of Teaching Resources in Psychology (OTRP) of the Society for Teaching of Psychology. She has taught both undergraduate and graduate courses at a wide range of institutions, including Lehman College (CUNY), Fordham University, and Teachers College, Columbia University. Her research examines risky behavior during adolescence and young adulthood, moral development, and ethics in research and teaching. She is the author of *The Psychology Major's Handbook,* co-author of *Careers in Psychology: Opportunities in a Changing World,* and maintains About Graduate School (http://gradschool.about.com), an Internet portal for applicants to graduate school, current graduate school, postdoctoral students, and new faculty. To learn more about Dr. Kuther's research, visit her website at http://tarakuther.com

GRADUATE STUDY IN PSYCHOLOGY

Your Guide To Success

By

TARA L. KUTHER

Western Connecticut State University

CHARLES C THOMAS • PUBLISHER, LTD.
Springfield • Illinois • U.S.A.

Published and Distributed Throughout the World by

CHARLES C THOMAS • PUBLISHER, LTD.
2600 South First Street
Springfield, Illinois 62704

ISBN 0-398-07478-X (hard)
ISBN 0-398-07479-8 (paper)

Library of Congress Catalog Card Number: 2003063363

With THOMAS BOOKS *careful attention is given to all details of manufacturing
and design. It is the Publisher's desire to present books that are satisfactory as to their
physical qualities and artistic possibilities and appropriate for their particular use.*
THOMAS BOOKS *will be true to those laws of quality that assure a good name
and good will.*

Printed in the United States of America
SR-R-3

Library of Congress Cataloging-in-Publication Data

Kuther, Tara L.
    Graduate study in psychology : your guide to success / by Tara L. Kuther.
       p. cm.
    Includes bibliographical references and index.
    ISBN 0-398-07478-X -- ISBN 0-398-07479-8 (pbk.)
    1. Psychology--Study and teaching (Graduate) I. Title.

BF77.K85 2004
15'0.71'1--dc22

                                                                        2003063363

PREFACE

Psychology is one of the most popular majors for undergraduate students today. Each year, more than 75,000 students in the United States earn bachelor's degrees in psychology. Many students consider graduate study, but are unsure of what it entails, what preparation it offers, and how to apply. As a professor of psychology, I've spent many hours in my office with students who were considering whether to go to graduate school. I've spent countless more hours researching the admissions process and providing advice about graduate school for the readers and subscribers of my website, About Graduate School, at About.com (http://gradschool.about.com). The advice in *Graduate Study in Psychology: Your Guide to Success* is largely derived from conversations and correspondence with my students and on-line readers.

This book will take you on an in-depth tour of the graduate admissions process. You'll learn how to decide whether graduate school is for you and how to apply to graduate school. We'll discuss:

- the differences between master's and doctoral programs
- differences among Ph.D. and Psy.D. degrees
- what graduate school is like
- how to locate graduate programs
- how to evaluate and choose programs
- what admissions committees look for in applicants
- how to improve your credentials for graduate school admission
- how to obtain research and applied experiences during college
- the timetable for applying to graduate school
- how to seek financial aid to fund graduate school
- the Graduate Record Exam
- how to write a compelling personal statement or admissions essay
- how to ask for letters of recommendation
- how to prepare for admissions interviews

- how to evaluate and accept offers
- what to do if you're rejected
- how to make the transition from college to graduate school
- how to succeed in graduate school

Each chapter of *Graduate Study in Psychology: Your Guide to Success* contains advice based on research, my own experiences as a professor, and tips from current graduate students. Boxes within each chapter present tips from students who've been there—successful students share what worked—as well as what didn't. The Appendix at the end of this book lists recommended readings and websites to help you at each stage of choosing, applying to, and succeeding in graduate school. Note that the websites are linked at my home page: http://tarakuther. com/grad/downloads.html Check the web page for frequently updated links and new resources. Also, as you progress through the admissions process, I invite you to share your experience, tips, and advice with me. Send an email to me at tk@tarakuther.com to share your graduate admissions experiences.

                                                        −Tara L. Kuther

ACKNOWLEDGMENTS

I am indebted to many who have assisted me in completing this project. Erin McDonald and Margarita Posada provided invaluable feedback on each chapter. I thank them for their time and their insight. I thank the students at Western Connecticut State University as well as my readers at About Graduate School (http://gradschool.about.com), for asking the questions that have helped me to articulate my thoughts about admission to graduate school. My parents, Philip and Irene Kuther, have been an instrumental source of support through my own graduate school years–thank you for encouraging my professional development, then and now. Larry DeCarlo, my husband, supports my work with patience, understanding, and love–thank you.

CONTENTS

                                                             Page

Preface v

Chapter

1. Considering Graduate School in Psychology and
Related Fields 3
   The Master's Degree 3
      What Does a Master's Degree Entail? 4
      Master's Degrees in Psychology and Related Fields 5
   The Doctoral Degree 9
      What Does a Doctoral Degree Entail? 9
      Ph.D. vs. Psy.D. 10
      Doctoral Specialties in Psychology .11
   What Is Graduate School Like? 17
      Doctoral Student Life 18
      Graduate School: The Good and the Bad 20
   Is Graduate School for You? 21
      Questions to Consider 21
      Reasons Not to Go to Graduate School 23
   Should You Work First? 23

2. Locating and Choosing Among Graduate Programs in
Psychology 26
   Locating Graduate Programs 26
      Understand Training Models 27
      Determine Your Goals 28
      Print Sources for Locating Graduate Programs 29
      Internet Sources for Locating Graduate Programs 30

Network to Locate Graduate Programs 31
Get Organized 31
Choose Programs 32
    First Criterion: Accreditation 33
    Second Criterion: Program Philosophy and Goals 34
    Third Criterion: Do Your Qualifications Match the
    Program's Prerequisites? 35
    Fourth Criterion: Faculty 35
    Additional Criteria for Evaluating Graduate Programs 36
Making Contact 40
Exhibit 1. Tips from Graduate Students 42

3. Preparing for Graduate School: Improving Your Credentials 43
    What Do Admissions Committees Look for? 43
        GPA and GRE Scores 44
        Letters of Recommendation 45
        Personal Statement 45
        Faculty Perspectives 46
        Secondary Admissions Criteria 47
    How Can You Improve Your Credentials? 48
        Your GPA 48
        Preferred Coursework 49
        Can You Raise Your GPA? 50
        What If It's Too Late? 51
    Practical Experience and Your Graduate School Application . .52
        Research Experience 52
        Field Experience 55
    Exhibit 2. Tips from Graduate Students 56

4. Overview of the Application Process 57
    Components of the Application 57
        Application Forms 57
        Personal Statement 58
        Graduate Admissions Examination (GRE) 59
        Transcripts 59
        Letters of Recommendation 60
        Curriculum Vitae 60

Overall Presentation 63

Preparing for Graduate Admissions: Timetable 64

Sophomore Year 64

Junior Year 66

Summer Before Your Senior Year 67

Senior Year, September 68

Senior Year, October 69

Senior Year, November 69

Senior Year, December 69

Senior Year, January 70

Senior Year, February 70

Senior Year, March/April 70

Financial Aid: How Will I Pay for Graduate School? 70

Requesting Aid 71

Teaching Assistantship 72

Research Assistantship 73

Exhibit 3. Sample Curriculum Vitae 74

Exhibit 4. Tips from Graduate Students 75

5. The Graduate Record Exam 77

The GRE General Test 77

GRE General Test Facts 78

When Should You Take the GRE General Test? 79

Verbal Section of the GRE 79

Quantitative Section of the GRE 80

Analytical Writing Section of the GRE 81

Scoring of the GRE 82

Preparing for the GRE General Test 83

Should You Ever Retake the GRE? 84

GRE Subject Test in Psychology 85

GRE Psychology Test Facts 85

Content of the GRE Psychology Test 86

Conquering Test Anxiety 86

Exhibit 5. Tips from Graduate Students 88

6. Personal Statements and Admissions Essays 89

Essay Topics: What Can You Expect to Write About? 90

On the Autobiographical Statement 91
Admissions Essay as Process 93
   Assess Yourself 93
   Review Your List of Programs 94
   Getting Started: Dealing with Writer's Block 94
   Remember to Respond to the Questions Posed 95
   Revising and Polishing Your Essay 95
Admissions Essay Tips 97
Exhibit 6. Questions to Consider as You Prepare Your Essay . .98
Exhibit 7. Tips from Graduate Students 99

7. Letters of Recommendation 101
   What Do Admissions Committees Request? 101
   Who To Ask? 102
   Who Not to Ask 104
   Approaching Referees 105
   What if You've Been out of School for a While? 106
   Provide Your Referees with Information 106
   About Confidentiality 107
   How to Get Good Letters of Recommendation 108
      Show Interest 108
      Enroll in Classes that Get You Noticed 108
      Participate in Class 109
      Get Research Experience 109
   Exhibit 8. Behaviors that Faculty Appreciate in Class 111
   Exhibit 9. What Not to Do: How to Irritate a Faculty
   Member 112
   Exhibit 10. Tips from Graduate Students 112

8. I've Submitted My Application: Now What? 114
   What to Expect 114
   Should You Make Contact? 115
      When to Make Contact 115
      When Not to Make Contact 116
   Waiting: What to Do Now? 117
   Hearing Back 118
   Exhibit 11. Tips from Graduate Students 118

9. The Interview 120
    Purpose of the Interview 120
    What to Expect 121
    Preparing for the Interview 121
    During the Interview 122
        Common Interview Questions 123
        What to Ask 125
        Interviewing Tips 127
        Managing Social Situations 128
    Stress Management: Coping with the Interview 128
    After the Interview 130
    Exhibit 12. Tips from Graduate Students 130

10. Decision Time 133
    Evaluating Offers and Graduate Programs 133
    Notifying Graduate Programs 134
    Being Wait-Listed 135
    Rejection 136
        Why Are Students Rejected? 137
        How to Proceed After Rejection 137
    Exhibit 13. Tips from Graduate Students 139

11. Transition to Graduate School 141
    Graduate School: A New Beginning 141
        Scope 141
        New Tasks 142
        Endless Reading 143
        De-Emphasis on Grades 143
        Emphasis on Professional Development 143
        Generating Knowledge 144
        Relationships Matter 144
        Establish Independence 145
        Politics 145
    Characteristics of Successful Students 146
    Your Relationship with Your Advisor and Mentor 147
        Differences Between Advisors and Mentors 147
        Choosing a Mentor 148

Take Your Advisor's Perspective 149
Understand the Other Side: Learn About Mentoring 150
Graduate Student Responsibilities 153
Easing Your Transition 154
Getting Organized: How Do You Begin? 155
Start a Research Journal 159
Deal with Stress 160
Exhibit 14. Tips from Graduate Students 162

Appendix: Recommended Readings and Web Resources 167
References 179
Index 181

GRADUATE STUDY IN PSYCHOLOGY
Your guide to success

Chapter 1

CONSIDERING GRADUATE SCHOOL IN PSYCHOLOGY AND RELATED FIELDS

Each year, over 74,000 students earn bachelor's degrees in psychology (National Center for Education Statistics, 2001). Although a bachelor's degree in psychology prepares graduates for a variety of careers, a graduate degree provides additional opportunities for professional advancement, respect, and financial security. By obtaining a graduate degree, you'll become an expert in your field. You'll gain the confidence and communication skills to disseminate what you've learned and improve your life and possibly the world around you.

Of course, graduate school isn't for everyone. Is it for you? How do you know? What is graduate school like? In this chapter we'll explore these questions and more. You'll learn about the various degrees that you may obtain through graduate study in psychology and related fields, how to decide if graduate school will advance your career, and how graduate school is different from college. If you're thinking about attending graduate school in psychology or a related field, your first step is to determine which degree is for you. You've got two basic choices: a master's degree or a doctoral degree. Let's take a closer look at master's and doctoral degrees.

THE MASTER'S DEGREE

The master's degree is shrouded by myth, as faculty often know little about master's degrees and master's-level careers (Actkinson, 2000). Despite faculty biases, master's degrees are very popular. About 13,000 students earn master's degrees in psychology each year (Hays-Thomas, 2000). Many more earn master's degrees in related fields like social work and counseling.

A master's degree will enable you to change career fields. For example, let's say that you've earned a bachelor's degree in English, but have decided that you want to become a counselor—complete a master's degree in counseling. You don't need a bachelor's degree in psychology to apply to graduate school in psychology and related fields. A master's degree will allow you to develop expertise in a new area and enter a new career. Typically, earning a master's degree requires two years of graduate study beyond the bachelor's degree, but those additional two years open the door to many career opportunities that are personally, professionally, and financially fulfilling. The most common master's degrees are the master of arts (M.A.) and master of science (M.S.). Note that whether you earn an M.A. or M.S. depends more on the school you attend than the academic requirements fulfilled; the two are different only in name, not in educational requirements or status. Master's degrees are offered in a variety of fields (e.g., psychology, mathematics, biology, etc.), just as bachelor's degrees are offered in many fields.

What Does a Master's Degree Entail?

Most master's degree programs in psychology require students to complete a master's thesis, or an extended research paper. In your master's thesis, you will pose a research question, review the relevant literature, and design and carry out a research study to address your question. More specifically, you'll identify a research question, use surveys, interviews, and other procedures to collect data about your question, analyze the data you've collected using statistics, draw conclusions, and make recommendations for future research. Some master's programs offer alternatives to the master's thesis, such as written comprehensive exams or other written projects that are less rigorous than theses. In service-oriented fields like clinical, counseling, and school psychology, master's degrees usually include a practicum, internship, or other applied experience (e.g., conducting therapy under supervision; Kuther & Morgan, 2004).

Master's Degrees in Psychology and Related Fields

If you're interested in helping people, you're not limited to a master's degree in psychology. There are a variety of other areas in which you can earn a master's degree and have the opportunity to work with people. Let's take a look at the range of master's options that may be of interest to psychology students.

Clinical and Counseling Psychology

A master's degree in clinical or counseling psychology prepares graduates to provide basic psychological services, including psychological assessments and therapy. Master's-level clinicians work in community mental health centers, schools, psychiatric hospitals, nonprofit organizations, and group practices. If you desire a master's degree in clinical or counseling psychology to establish an independent practice, recognize that master's level clinicians often must be supervised by licensed doctoral-level psychologists (Actkinson, 2000; Kuther & Morgan, 2004). In some states, master's clinicians meet requirements for licensure as a counselor or marriage and family therapist (discussed later in this chapter). Before enrolling in a master's program in clinical or counseling psychology, consider your interests and goals, and do your homework so that you're not surprised or disappointed later. Some alternatives to master's degrees in clinical and counseling psychology, such as social work, counseling, and marriage and family therapy, provide a greater range of practice opportunities than master's degrees in psychology.

School Psychology

A master's degree in school psychology prepares graduates to provide psychological services to children and adolescents within school settings. School psychologists assess students' learning aptitude, diagnose learning disabilities, assess special needs, and promote the overall development of children and adolescents (Himelein, 1999). School psychologists work with school personnel and with parents to determine classroom placements, to develop interventions to help deal with problematic behavior, and to promote adaptation within the school setting. Although many graduates obtain positions with master's degrees in school psychology, national certification as a school psychologist by the National Association of School Psychologists requires a specialist's degree, which is an advanced degree between the master's and doctoral degrees. The specialist's degree requires an additional year of graduate education beyond the master's degree, but will improve your competitiveness in the job market because three-quarters of nondoctoral-level school psychologists hold the specialist's degree (Himelein, 1999).

Industrial and Organizational Psychology

A master's degree in industrial/organizational psychology prepares graduates to apply psychological principles to the workplace. Industrial/organizational psychology training prepares graduates to engage in a variety of activities, including employee selection and placement, employee training and development, performance evaluation, policy formation and enforcement, team building, management advisement in issues of leadership and decision making, and organizational development (Kuther & Morgan, 2004). Master's degree holders in industrial/organizational psychology work in business, private organizations, corporate settings, and government.

Social Work

The master's degree in social work (M.S.W.) is a respected degree whose graduates are highly competitive for careers as therapists and clinicians in hospitals, clinics, schools, correctional facilities, nonprofit agencies, and private practice (Actkinson, 2000). Social workers help people to adapt and function in their everyday environments. A master's degree in social work requires two to three years of study (including training in human growth and development, social policies and programs, methods of practice, and social research) and a supervised internship of at least 900 hours of fieldwork. The M.S.W. allows degree-holders to practice therapy independently, as social workers are eligible for licensure or certification in all 50 states and the District of Columbia (U.S. Bureau of Labor Statistics, 2002).

Counseling

Although there are many different kinds of counselors (guidance counselor, career counselor, alcohol and drug abuse counselor, etc.), all work to help people who are experiencing problems or who need assistance in making decisions. For example, school or guidance counselors help students to evaluate their abilities and interests so that they can develop educational and vocational goals that are realistic and achievable. An employment counselor helps people to make career decisions and assists clients with aptitude testing, resume writing, and interviewing skills. An alcohol and drug abuse counselor assists clients in understanding their substance use patterns and overcoming addiction. Counselors work in a variety of settings including, schools, colleges, clinics, social agencies, correctional institutions, drug and alcohol rehabilitation centers, and private practice.

A master's degree in counseling entails two years of coursework and an internship of 700 to 900 hours, depending on state and graduate training. The master's degree in counseling enables graduates to seek licensure and practice therapy independently (varying by state). In 2001, 46 states and the District of Columbia had some form of required credentialing, licensure, or certification of counselors (U.S. Bureau of Labor Statistics, 2002). The exact requirements for independent practice vary by state, so do your homework to be sure that you will be prepared for the career you desire. Contact the National Board of Certified Counselors and Affiliates (http://www.nbcc.org) to learn about the counselor credentialing requirements in your state.

Occupational Therapy

Occupational therapists help people of all ages regain, develop, or master everyday skills in order to live independent, productive, and satisfying lives. For example, an occupational therapist might help a client with a physical disability learn how to perform critical daily routines, such as dressing, grooming, bathing, and eating. As the individual masters basic skills, the occupational therapist might assist him or her to develop higher-level skills needed to work outside the home. Occupational therapists are found in a variety of settings, including schools, hospitals, mental health centers, nursing homes, medical practices, home health agencies, and private practice.

If you're considering a career in occupational therapy, a master's degree, supervised internship, and passing score on a national exam are needed. Although it is currently possible to become an occupational therapist with a bachelor's degree, beginning in 2007, a master's degree will be the entry requirement (American Occupational Therapy Association, 2002). Even today, a master's degree will enhance your competitiveness for positions.

Marriage and Family Therapy

A master's degree in marriage and family therapy will prepare you for a career in helping families develop healthy patterns of interaction. Marriage and family therapists treat a wide range of serious clinical problems including depression, marital problems, anxiety, individual psychological problems, and child-parent problems; however, their emphasis in each of these situations is on the family. In other words, because the individual is part of a dynamic family system, marriage and family therapists argue that it isn't possible to treat the individual without considering the family. Marriage and family therapists are found in many environments, including inpatient facilities, employee assistance programs, health maintenance organizations, community mental health centers, schools, social service agencies, universities and research centers, courts, prisons, and private practice.

In order to practice as a marriage and family therapist, you'll need to be licensed in your state. Licensure requires earning a master's degree in marriage and family therapy (typically entailing two years of graduate study), completing two years of supervised practice, and earning a passing score on a national exam. Currently 44 states license or certify marriage and family therapists (American Association for Marriage and Family Therapy, 2002). As with the other degree options that we've discussed, research the requirements in your state to ensure that you're adequately prepared to seek licensure or certification.

Speech-Language Pathology

Speech pathologists assess and treat individuals with speech and language disorders. They diagnose the nature of the impairment, analyze speech and language irregularities, and devise treatment plans. Speech-language pathologists work with individuals who stutter, help people who have had strokes or experienced brain trauma to regain lost language and speech, and help children and adolescents who have language disorders to understand and give directions, convey ideas, and improve their language skills. Speech-language pathologists are found in schools, nursing homes, mental health centers, private practices, and medical settings. A master's degree in speech-language pathology, 300 to 375 hours of supervised clinical experience, and a passing score on a national examination are needed for licensure in most states.

Research Psychology

In addition to master's degrees in the professional areas that we've discussed, you might also consider a master's degree in research psychology, which offers preparation for a variety of other career opportunities for students. A master's degree in research-oriented fields such as quantitative psychology, developmental psychology, general psychology, or experimental psychology develops methodological, quantitative, and analytical skills that prepare students for research positions in university centers, government, business, and private organizations (Kuther & Morgan, 2004). A research-oriented master's degree provides training and experience in research and scholarship that may also serve as the first step towards a doctoral degree.

THE DOCTORAL DEGREE

Many students seek graduate degrees in psychology because of their desire to work with people. As we've seen, master's degrees in psychology enable degree holders to work directly with people, but in most cases require supervision by a licensed doctoral psychologist. There are several options for circumventing the need for supervision: (1) determine if your master's program meets the requirements for licensure as a counselor in your state; (2) seek a degree in counseling, social work, or marriage and family therapy; or (3) seek a doctoral degree.

What Does a Doctoral Degree Entail?

A doctoral degree in psychology usually entails five to seven years of graduate study, including research experience and supervised applied experience. During the first few years of graduate school, you'll take classes. You'll also work with a faculty member on his or her research and may even work as a teaching assistant. Your job during graduate school is to learn how to be a professional and create your own program of research. You'll read outside of class, consider research questions, and begin your own research program under your mentor's supervision. Most students are required to complete comprehensive examinations before they can begin working on their doctoral dissertations. Comprehensive exams are just that–written and sometimes oral examinations that require that you become well read and up-to-date with the latest research and theories in your field. Your dissertation is an in-depth research study that addresses a question pertinent to your research program. Most students take at least two years to complete their dissertations.

As you can see, obtaining a doctoral degree takes quite a chunk of time and is challenging, but is also rewarding. The doctoral degree will provide you with career flexibility and professional autonomy, but requires an extensive amount of time and commitment.

Ph.D. vs. Psy.D.

There are two different kinds of doctoral degrees: the Ph.D. and Psy.D. The Ph.D., or doctor of philosophy, like the master's degree, is offered in a variety of areas. Most of your college professors hold Ph.D. degrees in their chosen fields (e.g., anthropology, physics, mathematics, psychology). The Ph.D. is a research degree that entails coursework and research experience, including a doctoral dissertation. A dissertation is an extended academic paper that demonstrates your ability to undertake significant scholarship in your field. The Ph.D. dissertation requires that students complete an independent empirical research project that reflects a substantial contribution to the field and demonstrates the ability to build theory, test ideas, and/or discover new knowledge. You may obtain a Ph.D. in any of the psychological specialties discussed in this chapter. A Ph.D. in clinical or counseling psychology will entail supervised practical experience in addition to research and coursework requirements. With a Ph.D. in clinical or counseling psychology you will be eligible to apply for licensure in your state, as well as work in research and university settings.

The Psy.D., or doctor of psychology, is a professional degree meant for practitioners of psychology. It is offered only in clinical and counseling psychology and prepares graduates to practice psychology in therapeutic settings. The Psy.D. emphasizes professional training over research training. Graduates of Psy.D. programs become practicing psychologists and generally do not conduct research or work in university settings. The Psy.D. prepares graduates to be consumers of research, or to understand and apply research rather than generate it. Because of the applied and professional orientation of Psy.D. programs, dissertations typically do not entail empirical research. Instead, the Psy.D. dissertation demonstrates the student's ability to read and interpret a body of research literature and apply it in practical situations. For example, the dissertation may be a critique of the research literature in a specific area of psychology, a thorough analysis of a case using the psychological literature as a theoretical and empirical framework, or planning and evaluating a prevention or intervention program. While some have argued that a Ph.D. is more prestigious than a Psy.D., the two degrees prepare graduates for different careers. Choose the degree that will prepare you for the career you desire.

Doctoral Specialties in Psychology

As a student of psychology, you're already familiar with its breadth. Students who seek graduate-level careers in psychology have many options to choose from. Let's take a closer look at the many areas in which you may specialize.

Clinical Psychology

Clinical psychology is the study of emotional, behavioral, and psychological disorders. Specifically, clinical psychologists diagnose, treat, and conduct research on emotional, behavioral, and psychological disorders. For example, some clinical psychologists devise new assessment techniques for identifying persons suffering from psychological disorders. Others study the effectiveness of various forms of treatment for psychological disorders, such as new therapeutic techniques, medication, or behavioral management programs. You're probably familiar with the practitioner role of the psychologist from watching movies like

What About Bob? and *Analyze This.* In practice settings, clinical psychologists assess and treat people who are experiencing psychological problems and disorders that may range from normative difficulties, such as grief after losing a loved one or anxiety after being victimized by crime, to more serious and chronic disorders, such as schizophrenia, major depression, or bipolar disorder.

Counseling Psychology

Counseling psychology is similar to clinical psychology, but emphasizes the study of normative functioning and growth, rather than psychological distress. Counseling psychologists also work with people suffering from emotional, behavioral, and psychological disorders; however, the focus of counseling psychology is on the promotion of functioning, rather than treating pathology. Counseling psychologists study how to foster individual development and maximize skills, interests, and abilities to promote individual growth. For example, a counseling psychologist might examine how individuals cope with adversity and the factors that promote resilience in the face of disaster. Some counseling psychologists conduct therapy to help people adjust to everyday life issues and changes, such as divorce, remarriage, career shifts, and transitions to and from college. Others conduct vocational assessments and provide career guidance to help individuals select careers that match their interests and abilities. Counseling psychologists work in community settings such as mental health clinics, halfway houses, college counseling centers, and social service agencies, as well as health care settings, consulting firms, universities, and private practice. Like clinical psychologists, counseling psychologists practice, conduct research, and work as administrators in each of these settings.

Forensic Psychology

Forensic psychology and psychology and law represent the intersection of the fields of psychology and law. Some forensic psychologists conduct forensic evaluations for use as evidence in court cases (e.g., a forensic psychologist might assess the emotional impact of a traumatic injury) or to determine whether an individual is competent to stand trial. Other forensic psychologists conduct research that pertains to issues of law (e.g., the validity of eyewitness testimony or the effectiveness of various jury selection techniques). Some psychologists with interests in the law provide psychological services within correctional and police settings. Correctional psychologists assess inmates as they enter the prison system and maintain their psychological health throughout incarceration. Police psychologists provide a variety of services to law enforcement agencies, including selection and training of police officers, fitness for duty evaluations, organizational development and support, and counseling officers and their families to help them cope with the stressful lifestyle entailed by a career in law enforcement.

Most forensic psychologists hold doctoral degrees in clinical or counseling psychology and have completed predoctoral and postdoctoral internships in forensic, correctional, or police psychology (Kuther, 2004). Students with extensive interest in the law might consider a joint degree program that offers degrees in both psychology (Ph.D.) and the law (J.D.), which is an expensive and time consuming endeavor that prepares students to be both psychologists and lawyers. Recently, forensic psychology specialty programs also have emerged, offering doctoral degrees in forensic psychology; these specialty programs are new, so carefully research them and the types of careers they prepare you for before applying.

Health and Sport Psychology

Health psychologists study how biopsychosocial factors (or the interaction of factors at the biological or physical level, psychological level, and social level) influence health, illness, and wellness. Sport psychologists examine the influence of psychological factors on physical and athletic functioning. Sport psychologists don't limit themselves to the study of sports but rather include all types of physical activity or exercise. Both health and sport psychologists may be involved in service delivery, college or university teaching, or research.

In practice settings, health psychologists collaborate with other health care professionals such as physicians, dentists, nurses, physician's assistants, dietitians, social workers, pharmacists, and physical and occupational therapists to provide comprehensive health care (Kuther & Morgan, 2004). They engage in assessment, treatment, and research activities to diagnose and understand health, wellness, and illness, as well as prevent and intervene when needed to promote health and assist people with health problems. Practicing and research-oriented health psychologists develop and evaluate prevention and intervention programs to help people learn more healthy habits and adjust to health problems. Health psychologists are found in medical settings, colleges and universities, corporations, and governmental public health agencies, and private practice.

In practice, sport psychologists apply psychological principles (e.g., imagery, visualization, relaxation, goal setting, self-talk) to help athletes and performers perform at their best. Sport psychologists who practice are found in university counseling centers, sports medicine clinics, consulting agencies, and private practice. Other sport psychologists engage in research within university, medical research, business, or government settings. Sport psychology research examines how athletic participation influences health throughout the life span, as well as what factors influence our ability to engage in physical activity.

Health and sport psychologists complete a doctoral degree in psychology (usually in clinical or counseling psychology, but sometimes other areas of psychology) and then specialize in health or sport psychology during the supervised internship and postdoctoral training. There are also a growing number of doctoral programs specifically in health and sport psychology; these are new programs and their emphases are diverse, so research them carefully to be sure that you understand their training emphases.

Physiological Psychology

Physiological psychologists or biopsychologists study human functioning and the relationship between biology and behavior (e.g., How do we see? How do hormones affect our behavior?). A doctoral degree in physiological psychology or biopsychology is a research degree that prepares graduates for teaching and research careers in academia. Physiological psychologists also conduct research in government settings, for example, at government research facilities like the Centers for Disease Control or the National Institutes of Health. Others work in private industry; a physiological psychologist might develop and test new drugs for a pharmaceutical company.

Neuropsychology

Neuropsychologists or clinical neuropsychologists study the nervous system and develop and apply psychological and neurological assessments and interventions to assist clients suffering from brain dysfunction (e.g., a patient suffering memory loss following a traumatic brain injury). In practice settings, neuropsychologists diagnose the extent of brain damage or severity of impairment in clients. Neuropsychologists are employed in applied settings such as medical hospitals, and clinics and private practice, as well as in academic and research positions.

Neuropsychologists often are trained as generalists in clinical or counseling doctoral programs, then complete extensive training in neuroscience during internship and postdoctoral study. In recent years, several doctoral programs in neuropsychology have emerged. As with all programs, research these carefully to determine whether they will prepare you for licensure in your state and for the career that you desire.

Experimental Psychology

Experimental psychologists specialize in conducting research and tend to develop extensive skills in research methodology. Experimental psychologists apply their research skills to their topical area of interest (e.g., learning, sensation, perception, human performance, motivation, memory, language, thinking, and communication). For example, some experimental psychologists specialize in studying cognition: how we take in, use, store, retrieve, and apply information. Others study sensation and perception, or how we use our senses to understand the world around us. A doctoral degree in experimental psychology prepares graduates for careers as professors in colleges and universities, and researchers in academia, industry, and government (Kuther & Morgan, 2004).

Quantitative Psychology and Psychometrics

Quantitative psychologists, also called mathematical psychologists, study research methods and statistics. They are specialists in conducting research (e.g., designing experiments, conducting statistical analyses, and interpreting the results of experiments). Some quantitative psychologists specialize in psychometrics, the science of measuring human characteristics. Psychometricians are measurement specialists who devise and test ways of measuring people's behavior, abilities, potential, and functioning. For example, a psychometrician might devise and test a new measure of intelligence. A doctoral degree in quantitative psychology or psychometrics prepares graduates for careers as professors in colleges and universities, researchers in academia, industry, and government, as well as number-crunching, problem-solving, and computer-oriented careers in business and industry (Kuther & Morgan, 2004).

Developmental Psychology

Developmental psychologists study how we change throughout our lives, from conception to infancy, childhood, adolescence, young adulthood, middle adulthood, old age, and death. Most developmental psychologists specialize in a particular age group (e.g., adolescents or infants). The fastest growing area within developmental psychology today is gerontology, of the study of aging and older adulthood (i.e., How do we age? What is successful aging and how do we promote it?).

A growing number of developmental psychologists, called applied developmental psychologists, are concerned with applying knowledge from developmental psychology to solve practical problems as well as to develop and evaluate prevention and intervention programs that promote growth and development (e.g., Head Start). Applied developmental psychologists work to educate the public about important findings in developmental psychology. They provide information to policy makers, businesses, industry, healthcare professionals, and parents. Some applied developmental psychologists provide direct services to individuals by administering and interpreting developmental assessments (i.e., tests to measure an individual's pattern of cognitive, emotional, physical, or social growth), developing behavioral management programs for individuals and groups, and delivering psychological services in various mental health settings (e.g., group therapy; Fisher & Osofsky, 1997; University of New Orleans, 2001). Developmental psychologists and applied developmental psychologists are found in university settings, research settings, and applied settings, such as hospitals, social service agencies, mental health clinics, and schools. Developmental psychologists are also found in advertising, product design (e.g., toys), and marketing research careers (Kuther & Morgan, 2004).

Social Psychology

Social psychologists study social interaction: How we interact with each other and the world around us. Social psychologists study personality (e.g., Why do we act the way that we do?), attitude formation and change, and interpersonal relations such as attraction, prejudice, group dynamics, and aggression. A doctoral degree in social psychology prepares graduates for academic and research careers, as well as for nontraditional careers in marketing research, advertising, and media consultation (Kuther & Morgan, 2004). Now that you've had an opportunity to consider some of the many degree options and fields open to students who are interested in psychology, we'll take a closer look at the graduate school experience.

WHAT IS GRADUATE SCHOOL LIKE?

Our first stop on our journey through the graduate application process entails ensuring that you're aware of what's in store should you attend graduate school. So what is graduate school really like? Well, that depends on what degree you're seeking. Master's programs are often similar to undergraduate programs. You'll take classes in which you read, hear lectures, engage in class discussions, complete exams, and write papers. You may also complete comprehensive exams, exams that are designed to test your knowledge of your field (and therefore assess your entire graduate education) and a thesis or an empirical study. Typically an advisor is assigned to you and you are awarded credits toward your degree for completing your master's thesis. Some programs even have several master's thesis courses in which enrolled students are guided through the thesis process in a structured manner. High levels of structure make most master's programs similar to your experiences as an undergraduate. At the doctoral level, things are very different.

Doctoral Student Life

To begin, doctoral programs are generally less structured than college. You must figure out a way to get along and work with your advisor, carve out an area of research, find a dissertation topic, and make the professional contacts that are essential to advancing in your field and getting a job after graduation. It's up to you to find your way. The sudden burst of independence can be overwhelming for students. All too often new graduate students wait for someone to tell them what to do. The longer they wait without answers or direction, the more fearful they become about their futures. Needless to say, stress and fear aren't conducive to studying and success in graduate school. Conquer your fears by learning about graduate school now, while you've got time to prepare and decide if it's really for you. So, what's in store for you if you enroll in a doctoral program?

Classes

At least in Ph.D. programs, graduate school is not merely a series of classes. Sure you'll take classes during the first couple of years, but your later years will emphasize research (and you probably won't take any classes during those later years). The purpose of graduate school is to master your discipline through independent reading and study, so you'll take fewer classes in graduate school than you did in college. You'll also be encouraged to read and study within your areas of interest. For example, when I was a graduate student in developmental psychology, we were encouraged to focus our studies on our area of interest. So since I was interested in adolescence, I directed my reading and assignments toward fulfilling my need to learn about adolescent development; my paper for the required Psychology and Law course examined adolescents' abilities to provide informed consent for abortion (as well as the relevant law); in my Social Cognition course I wrote a paper examining the development of moral reasoning during adolescence, and so on.

Apprenticeship Model

If you're considering graduate school because you're doing well in college and like school, be aware that graduate school is essentially an apprenticeship. Most of what you learn in graduate school will not come from classes, but from other activities, like doing research and attending conferences. You'll work closely with a faculty member on his or her research. As an apprentice of sorts, you'll learn how to define research problems, design and carry out research studies to test your hypotheses, and disseminate your results. The end goal is to become an independent scholar and design your own research program.

Research Rules

While college centered around classes, doctoral programs emphasize research. Yes, you'll take courses, but the purpose of graduate school is to learn to do research. The emphasis is on learning how to gather information and construct knowledge independently. For example, often instead of taking courses in a given subject, you'll go to the library, research it, and read about it on your own. That's preparation for a career in research. As a researcher or professor, much of your job will consist of gathering materials, reading it, thinking about it, and designing studies to test your ideas about a given phenomenon. Doctoral programs offer preparation for a career in research, while master's programs emphasize application of research (e.g., understanding it and applying it).

It's a Job

Instead of sitting in class for a couple of hours a day and then being free to play, graduate school is more like a job that occupies all of your time. When you enroll in a doctoral program, you'll spend a great deal of your time working on research in your advisor or mentor's lab. This means that you'll need to approach graduate school as a full-time job; it's not "school" in the undergraduate sense. If you soared through college with little studying, you're in for a big culture shock. The reading lists will be longer and more extensive than you've encountered in college. More importantly, you'll be expected to read and be prepared to critically evaluate and discuss it all. Most graduate programs require that you take initiative for your learning and demonstrate commitment to your career. Remember that no one will hold your hand and walk you through. You must provide your own motivation.

You Won't Finish Quickly

This isn't meant to discourage you, but to provide you with a realistic perspective. Typically a doctoral program is a five- to eight-year commitment. Usually the first year is the most structured year, entailing classes and lots of reading. Students usually must pass a set of comprehensive exams at various points in the program to continue. For example, in my graduate program, students took a set of comprehensive exams at the end of the first year to receive their master's degrees and then another set after completing all coursework (at the end of the third year) to progress to doctoral candidate status. There is often a great deal of stress associated with these exams.

As you progress in graduate school, you'll become more involved in research and often also in teaching, serving as a teaching assistant, and later, as a course instructor. You'll spend a great deal of time searching for a thesis topic and advisor, and then reading up on your topic to prepare your dissertation proposal. Once the proposal is accepted by your dissertation committee (typically composed of five faculty who you and your advisor have chosen based on their knowledge of the field), you're free to begin your research study. You'll plug away for months or even years in some cases until you've conducted your research, made some conclusions, and written it all up. Then comes your defense: You'll present your research to your dissertation committee, answering questions, and supporting the validity of your work. If all goes well, you'll walk away with a new title and some funky letters behind your name: Ph.D.

Graduate School: The Good and the Bad

So, we've seen what graduate school is all about. Now, why should you do it? Are there benefits to graduate study? One important benefit is that you are able to spend all day thinking about something that you find fascinating (i.e., your research topic). It's amazing to conduct research to solve problems and discover things that no one has before. The intellectual stimulation of graduate study is unmatched, but there are also some negative aspects. It's hard! Devising methods of testing your ideas requires creativity and determination because designing experiments and research studies isn't as easy as it appears in undergraduate textbooks.

A major downside to attending graduate school is that it entails a huge time commitment. Research will take on a new meaning: your life will be devoted to your work. In college, work may have been one of the many activities that you've spent time doing (e.g., class work in other areas, volunteer activities, sports, work, etc.). In graduate school your world changes. Most of your interactions will be with other scientists and there will be little time for outside activities. Chapter 11 provides more information about what graduate school is like and how to navigate the transition to this new world. You might skim a few pages now to get a feel for what you're in for, should you decide to apply to graduate school.

IS GRADUATE SCHOOL FOR YOU?

How do you know if graduate school is right for you? Answering this question requires brutal honesty on your part and will take time, so allow yourself a few weeks or even months to make your decision. As you realize by now, your decision to attend graduate school is serious because graduate study entails significant amounts of time, energy, financial strain, and emotional strain. Carefully consider if it is right for you and fits in with your interests and goals.

Graduate school is probably a good choice for you if you know where you'd like to go in terms of your career and graduate study is necessary for that career. For example, college teaching and research, and independent practice are careers in which graduate education is required. You must love your field and seek to immerse yourself in your work. Passion is essential because you'll be spending many years studying, doing research, and working in your discipline. If you're not passionate now, graduate study will certainly not improve your disposition. Grad school is not the place to find yourself or discover your interests. Rather, in graduate school you're expected to have clearly defined interests and goals.

Questions to Consider

Take time to consider the following questions to determine if graduate school is right for you. It's soul-searching time. Delving deep into your psyche to critically evaluate your interest, abilities, and goals often is unpleasant, but essential to making a choice you can live with for the next two to seven years.

- What do you want to accomplish in your life?
- What are your short- and long-term professional goals?
- Is graduate study essential to reaching these goals?
- Is a master's or doctorate best for obtaining your goals?
- What will you specialize in?
- Do you have the interests and abilities to succeed?
- Are you delaying your career planning by seeking graduate study?
- Will graduate study and the financial, personal, and emotional burdens ultimately enable you greater career possibilities and mobility?
- Are you motivated enough to study for two to seven years or more?
- Can you take the pressure?
- Can you afford it? Can you find the money to pay for tuition, books, and living expenses?
- Are you willing to meet the extensive research, coursework, and major paper demands of another academic program?
- Would continuing education alternatives (like college courses, vocational school and community college courses, or professional seminars and workshops) be more appropriate in achieving your goals?

A large part of this decision rests on whether you have the academic and personal qualities needed for success in graduate school. As Kuther (2003) points out, "self-reliance, a desire to excel, commitment to scholarship, intellectual curiosity, and emotional stability are necessary to successfully navigate the rigor, stress, and often impersonal nature of graduate school"(p. 171). Generally the following academic and personal skills will enhance your chances for success in graduate school: writing and communication skills, research skills, discipline, stress management skills, social skills (i.e., ability to establish a relationship with a mentor and peers), time management skills, the ability to delay gratification, and maturity. Determining whether you have the necessary skills to succeed is difficult and requires honesty and the ability to look inward and critically evaluate yourself. Also seek input from outside sources, such as your professors. Professors have been through graduate school and can tell you what it's really like and what qualities are needed for success.

Reasons Not to Go to Graduate School

Students choose graduate school for a wide variety of reasons, including intellectual curiosity and professional advancement. Unfortunately, some students attend graduate school because they aren't sure what to do with their lives or don't feel ready for a job. These aren't good reasons. Graduate school requires an intense commitment of time and money. If you're not sure that you're ready, then it's best to wait.

Don't attend graduate school because you're afraid or think you have no other options. Grad school won't offer you an easy way out or a release from adult life. Remember that graduate study is part of a career plan and eventually you'll have to search for a job; don't use grad school to extend your play time. Don't attend graduate school because you think that there's nothing you can do with your major. A college degree provides you with many skills that are highly valued in the workplace, such as research and analysis, critical thinking, and communications.

Don't attend graduate school because you feel it's expected of you: Do it for yourself, not for others. Graduate school isn't right for a surprising amount of students who enter graduate study, many of whom fail to complete their degrees. Take the time to think through this decision because it must be your own.

SHOULD YOU WORK FIRST?

Should you take time off before graduate study? This is a personal decision and there's no definitive right or wrong answer. However, if you have doubts about your educational and career aspirations don't be afraid to take time to rethink your goals. If you're certain that graduate study is for you but still want to take a break, consider your reasons for taking time off.

Are you tired? Exhaustion is understandable. After all, you've just spent 16 or more years in school. If this is your primary reason for taking time off, consider whether your fatigue will ease over the summer.

You've got two or three months off before graduate school starts; can you rejuvenate? Depending on the program and degree, graduate school takes anywhere from three to eight or more years to complete. If you're certain that graduate school is in your future and if you're concerned about time, perhaps you shouldn't wait.

There are also many good reasons for taking time off before applying to graduate school. If you feel unprepared for graduate school, a year off may enhance your application. For example, you might take a prep-course for the GRE or other standardized tests required for admission. Improving your scores on standardized tests will enhance your chances of being accepted to the program of your choice. Perhaps more importantly, financial aid in the form of scholarships and awards are distributed based on standardized test scores.

You might also seek research experience during your time off to further enhance your application. Maintain contacts with the faculty at your undergraduate institution and seek research experiences with them. Such opportunities are beneficial because they let faculty members get to know you and thereby write more personal letters of recommendation. Plus you'll gain insight into what it's like to work in your field.

Another reason students sometimes take a year or two off between undergraduate and graduate school is to obtain work experience. Some fields, such as nursing and business, recommend and expect some work experience. In addition, the financial lure and the opportunity to save money is hard to resist. Graduate school is expensive and it's unlikely that you'll be able to work many hours, if any, while you're in school, so some students take a year off to fatten their bankbooks in preparation for a few lean years of graduate study.

Many students worry whether they'll return to school after a year or two away from the grind. That's a realistic concern, but don't hesitate to take the time that you need to be sure that graduate school is right for you. Graduate school requires a great deal of motivation and the ability to work independently. Generally, students who are more interested and committed to their studies are more likely to be successful. Time off may increase your desire and commitment to your goals.

Finally, recognize that attending graduate school several years after completing a bachelor's degree is not unusual. More than one-half of graduate students in the United States are over age 30. If you wait before going to grad school, be prepared to explain your decision, what you learned, and how it improves your candidacy. Time off can be beneficial if it enhances your credentials and prepares you for the stresses and strains of graduate school.

Chapter 2

LOCATING AND CHOOSING AMONG GRADUATE PROGRAMS IN PSYCHOLOGY AND RELATED FIELDS

So, you've decided to do it! How do you start your graduate application odyssey? It's easy to feel overwhelmed and confused because there are thousands of graduate programs in psychology. In this chapter we'll talk about how to navigate your way through the vast amounts of information to learn about, evaluate, and choose the graduate programs to which you'll apply.

LOCATING GRADUATE PROGRAMS

Now that you've decided that graduate school is for you, don't delay in beginning the arduous process of preparing your application. The first step is preparing a list of possible programs to which you may apply. Although this is the first step, it's a very important task because it's from this list that you'll cull the programs to which you'll ultimately apply and possibly attend. Gaining admission to a graduate program in psychology is very difficult; most programs get from two to 50 times as many applicants as they have openings. Plan to apply to at least eight to ten programs (and more if you're aiming for a slot in a clinical or counseling psychology doctoral program). Cast your net wide and expect to gather initial information from 30 to 40 programs at this stage. Later in this chapter we'll talk about how to narrow your choices, but our task now is to locate the wide range of possibilities for graduate study.

Understand Training Models

Before you begin your search for graduate programs, understand that there are three basic models of training within psychology. Choose a model that fits your interests—and then choose programs that emulate your chosen model. This step is important because most psychologists engage in the same type of activities that they experienced in their graduate program of study (Kuther, 2003).

Research-Scientist Model

The research-scientist model is oriented towards creating scientists—scholars who will make new discoveries and advance psychological knowledge. The research-scientist model is the oldest training model and it characterizes most programs in the core academic areas of psychology such as experimental, social/personality, quantitative, physiological, and developmental psychology. Graduates trained as research-scientists conduct original research, teach, and write about their research findings. The emphases of training include experimental methods, methodological skill, and content knowledge. Graduates trained as research-scientists tend to be employed as college and university professors, and researchers at universities, government, and industry settings.

Scientist-Practitioner Model

Scientist-practitioner models of graduate training mold students into scholars who integrate their research training with applied work. This model is commonly found in programs in clinical, counseling, school, and industrial psychology. The scientist-practitioner model entails training in research and methodology, like the research-scientist model, but the scientist-practitioner model also entails courses in applied areas as well as internships and practica. Graduates trained in the scientist-practitioner model are employed by hospitals and clinical practices, teach in colleges and universities, and own private practices. The extent to which a particular psychologist engages in both research and practice depends on his or her job setting and commitment to research; most practicing clinicians do little to no research.

Professional Psychologist/Practitioner Model

Graduate programs oriented towards the professional psychologist/practitioner model train students to provide psychological services. Most Psy.D. programs are guided by the professional psychologist/practitioner model, which emphasizes clinical practice over research. Graduates are trained to be consumers of research rather than producers of it–and tend to be employed in practice settings such as hospitals, clinics, and private practice.

Determine Your Goals

Whereas an undergraduate major is a broad introduction to a given field, graduate education is very narrow and specialized. In psychology, you'll have to choose a specialization such as experimental, clinical, counseling, developmental, social, or biological psychology. This decision must be made early because it will determine the scope of your research and the programs to which you'll apply.

So, before you begin researching graduate programs consider your career objectives, long-term aspirations, and goals. Do you see yourself as a researcher, clinician, or industry professional? In what types of work settings do you envision yourself? What professional activities are you drawn to? In what area of psychology would you like to specialize? In choosing a specialization, consider your interests. What courses did you especially like? On what topics have you written papers? Many students know that they're interested in psychology but have a hard time determining in what area to specialize. If you're not sure of what career path to take, the book, *Careers in Psychology: Opportunities in a Changing World,* by myself and Robert Morgan (2004), might be helpful because it provides an overview of career opportunities within each subdiscipline of psychology. Also seek advice from professors about the differences among the various specialties in a given field. Inquire about existing employment opportunities for each specialization. Look back over the descriptions of subfields and graduate degrees in Chapter 1 and try to imagine yourself working in each field. How do you think it would feel? Would it make you happy? Would it interest you for a lifetime? What training model, scientist, practitioner, or scientist-practitioner, will prepare you for your desired career?

Think very carefully about the questions we've discussed and then write down your answers to create a written profile of your desired graduate program. Specifically, you'll need to identify the following:

- area of psychology in which to specialize
- degree option that best meets your goals
- professional activities in which you plan to engage
- training model that best fits your goals

Now that you have these initial criteria laid out, you can begin your search for graduate programs.

Print Sources for Locating
Graduate Programs

The *Peterson's Guide to Graduate and Professional Programs* contains descriptions of nearly every graduate program within North America. The *Peterson's Guide* is a multiple volume set; for graduate programs in psychology, examine the volume entitled *Social Sciences & Social Work*. You'll get basic program information such as the areas of expertise of faculty, number of faculty, and who to contact for more information. You can find the *Peterson's Guide* in nearly every college and public library. Be sure to bring a pen and paper to take notes on all of the programs that you discover.

Another resource that you may find helpful for locating graduate programs is the *Graduate School Decision Guide,* published by the Educational Testing Service. The *Decision Guide* is a multiple volume set; psychology students will be interested in the volume entitled *Graduate Programs in Psychology.* The *Decision Guide* is organized by state, lists institutions and provides basic information for each, including the degrees offered, specializations, and number of students, as well as information about requirements, such as admissions tests, undergraduate majors, and recommendation letters.

If you're specifically interested in clinical or counseling psychology, the *Insider's Guide to Graduate Programs in Clinical & Counseling Psychology* will be a useful reference. It's published every two years and contains lists of doctoral programs accredited by the American Psychological Association. A profile of each program is provided, including the acceptance rate, theoretical orientation of the program, the program's emphasis on research and clinical practice, and admission requirements. The volume also includes some general information about applying to graduate school.

The American Psychological Association publishes the most useful of the graduate school guides, entitled *Guide to Graduate Study in Psychology*. Updated every two years, the *Guide to Graduate Study in Psychology* describes each graduate program in psychology within North America. It's organized alphabetically by state and provides the following information for each school: criteria for admission, program emphasis, number of faculty members, enrollments, and average GPA and GRE scores of new students. Like each of the other guides mentioned, the *Guide to Graduate Study in Psychology* is available at most university and public libraries.

Internet Sources for Locating Graduate Programs

In addition to printed sources of information, use the Internet to locate information about graduate programs. Most universities have web pages designed to attract potential students. The amount of information that you'll find on a university website will vary. Some universities put their entire course catalogue online and others just offer a brief program overview. Try to locate the web page. Some departments (unfortunately not all) have elaborate pages that explain the program and resources in detail. You'll often find links to faculty web pages where you can find information about faculty members' research. The one caveat to gathering information about graduate programs from the web is that web pages are not always current. Be sure to look for a date when the web page was last updated (usually this information is provided at the very bottom of the page).

How do you find a university or department web page? Use a search engine like Yahoo.com or Google.com. Enter in your search terms (like "graduate programs and psychology," or the name of a particular university) and you'll get a list of links to web pages that match your keywords. You can also examine the list of links to graduate programs in psychology that I maintain at About.com's About Graduate School site (http://gradschool.about.com/cs/psychprograms/).

Network to Locate Graduate Programs

Don't forget the "human element" when searching for graduate programs. Talk to your professors about your area of interest and ask for their suggestions. Professors can provide you with advice based on their experience, give advice about programs that meet your interests, and possibly even recommend people with whom you should study. Professors can provide you with information about how you measure up to former students who've attended graduate school. They also might identify colleagues at other schools who you should contact. Speak with recent graduates from your department who are enrolled in graduate school to get advice and insights about what graduate school is really like.

GET ORGANIZED

Now that you have an initial list of potential programs, contact each and request applications and course catalogs. You often can request this information from a university website–and some schools already have this information available on their websites.

As you gather materials from each program, stay organized–difficult as it might be. Applying to graduate school is a stressful endeavor. One way to help you manage the stress is to retain some control over the process. While you can't control the admissions committee, you can control how you approach the application process and the quality of your application. Set up an organizational system to manage the great load of application materials that will come your way and you'll get a better idea of the task ahead of you. Let's take a closer look at how to get organized.

First, carefully read everything. Requirements vary from program to program, so read each application thoroughly. After this initial reading, if you have the impression that the program isn't a good fit for you (based on your career goal and interests) or that it's unlikely that you qualify for admission (based on your GPA and GRE scores, and other experiences), then strike the program from your list.

Organize graduate school materials as they arrive. Use folders to sort your admissions materials–one folder per program. On the front cover of the folder, print the name of the program and school, date the application is due, required test scores, number of recommendation letters, and the number and types of essays. Organize your folders within a filing cabinet, file crate, or sturdy cardboard box so that all the material is easily accessible and won't get lost. It's easy to procrastinate and put this task off until later, so force yourself to carefully read application materials and organize them as they arrive rather than waiting. This method will help you to see the scope of the task that lies ahead and will reduce your anxiety by providing a sense of organization and control.

Once you've sorted your collection of application and admissions materials, your next step is to determine whether you have all of the information necessary to make decisions about each program. For each program, make sure that you have the following information:

- Type of training that's offered
- Course sequence
- Practica and applied experiences offered
- Names of faculty and their research interests and areas of expertise
- Housing opportunities
- Financial aid opportunities

If you're missing any pieces of information, check the program website and, if necessary, contact the admissions office. Remember to be polite and professional when contacting programs to which you might apply.

CHOOSE PROGRAMS

Although the admissions committee will evaluate you to determine if you have the potential to excel in graduate school, remember that you also have an evaluative role in this process. Your job is to carefully examine each graduate program to determine whether it fits your interests and needs. That's an important point that is sometimes lost on students. I've heard students explain that they'll choose the program that chooses them, but that's not the best attitude to have about the admissions process. Getting into graduate school is certainly a competitive and stressful process; however, it's important to be an educated consumer. Carefully evaluate each program to determine if it fits your needs. Begin evaluating programs before you send in your applications because your research might change your mind about applying to a particular program, and perhaps more importantly, might better inform your application and make it more likely to lead to success.

As you research graduate programs, you'll notice that programs differ in goals, training philosophies, theoretical orientations, facilities, and resources. How well does each match your career goals and aspirations? How well does each program fulfill your expectations of what graduate training should entail? As you begin to evaluate programs and narrow your selections, consider each of the following elements, in the order presented:

First Criterion: Accreditation

Note that this criterion, APA accreditation, only applies to clinical, counseling, and school psychology programs. Nonpractitioner programs, like experimental, physiological, developmental, cognitive, and other research-oriented programs are not subject to accreditation. So, if you're planning on applying to clinical, counseling, or school psychology programs, carefully evaluate whether your chosen programs meet this criterion, but if you're applying to programs in other areas of psychology, skip ahead to the next criterion.

Now, what is APA accreditation? The American Psychological Association (APA) is a national association of psychologists and one of its activities is to evaluate practice-oriented psychology programs to ensure that the educational criteria meet the public's needs. APA accredits doctoral programs only in the practice areas of clinical, school, and counseling psychology. In order to be accredited, a program must meet the minimum standards for clinical training established by APA, which includes criteria such as faculty credentials, specific coursework, eligibility for state licensure, research and clinical opportunities, and internships. A site visit confirms that these requirements are met, and they must be maintained over time.

If you are applying to clinical, counseling, or school programs, be sure that the programs are accredited because a degree from an APA-approved program carries more weight; students from accredited programs are more successful in competing for clinical internships and jobs. Perhaps more important, many states *require* doctoral degrees from APA programs for licensure so if you attend a graduate program in clinical, counseling, or school psychology that is not accredited, you may not be eligible for licensure (and thus the ability to practice) in your state. Do your homework now to avoid wasting your time and money.

Second Criterion: Program Philosophy and Goals

Graduate programs don't fly by the seat of their pants in training students. Instead, they have mission statements, program philosophies, and goals that guide their choices of training activities. You can find information about the department and program goals for students within the admissions materials, department or program brochure, and on the department or program website. Do the program's goals complement your own? Through your research, you should know the answers to the following questions:

- Is the department heavily research-oriented, theoretical, or applied?
- Does the program emphasize theory, practice, or both?
- Is the program oriented towards producing researchers?
- What training model does the program employ (e.g., researcher-scientist, scientist-practitioner, or professional psychologist-practitioner)?
- What's the program's theoretical orientation (e.g., cognitive-behavioral, psychoanalytic)?
- Is the program well established or relatively new?

Examining the program philosophy and goals is important because programs that offer the same degree can be very different in terms of the types of training they offer and the types of specialists they are designed to create. For example, two developmental psychology programs may have very different emphases (e.g., child development versus life span development, or traditional experimental research verses applied research and program evaluation). Your ultimate qualifications will depend heavily on the graduate training you obtain, so ask questions and gather information to ensure that you choose graduate programs that will prepare you for the career you seek.

Third Criterion: Do Your Qualifications Match the Program's Prerequisites?

Compare each program's prerequisites or stated criteria for admission, including grade point average, GRE scores, and coursework, with your own qualifications to assess your match or fit to the program. You'll notice that your qualifications exceed the stated requirements for some graduate programs; these programs are *strong bets* or "safety programs" for which you're likely to gain admission. For other programs, either your grade point average or GRE scores might exceed the lower limit provided, but perhaps not the higher. Such programs are *good bets* because you meet all of the criteria, but do not exceed it. Other programs might be classified as *long shots* because your grades or GRE might not meet the stated criteria; don't apply to too many long shots because your chances of gaining admission are small (but possible). Finally, you may find that you don't meet two or more of the stated criteria for some programs–these should be omitted from your list because it's very unlikely that you'd gain admission (American Psychological Association, 1997).

Fourth Criterion: Faculty

Faculty members are the pillars of a graduate program–they make or break a program. Consider the faculty members of each program you research: Who are they? Do they publish often and in refereed journals (recent publications often are listed on department and faculty web pages; also search PsychInfo or other article databases to learn of faculty publications). Gather information on the following items to learn more about a graduate program's faculty:

- What are the faculty members' research interests? Do they match yours?
- What is the ratio of faculty to students?
- If you're considering applied programs, such as clinical or counseling programs, do faculty members have applied experience?
- What are faculty members' credentials?
- What awards, grants, and special recognition have they earned?
- Does the department have nationally or internationally known scholars in the field?

- Do the top scholars in the program teach, or are they primarily involved in research (you can learn this by examining the course offerings and course catalogue, often available online)?
- Conduct a literature search on faculty members whose work interests you. Do they publish? Read some abstracts to learn more about their work.

Additional Criteria for Evaluating Graduate Programs

Accreditation, program mission or philosophy, match to your own qualifications, and faculty members are the most important bases for evaluating graduate programs at this stage in the admissions process. However, there are a variety of other criteria that you should use in determining to which programs to apply, and more importantly, which program ultimately to attend. Let's examine them.

Coursework and Teaching Style

Examine the curriculum. What courses are required of students? Look over the course descriptions to get a feel of what you'll learn in the program. Does the program provide applied experiences such as practica or internships? Is the curriculum structured or flexible? Try to find information about specific courses; you often can find this information online. Faculty web pages often include links to syllabi and course assignments. Carefully examine these pages to learn more about what it's like to be a student in the program. Given everything you've learned from examining the department and faculty web pages, as well as the admissions materials, how student-oriented would you rate the program? Unfortunately some graduate programs emphasize faculty research over the education of graduate students. Your job is to try to determine how important education is to the department faculty—it's very difficult to assess from afar, but faculty web pages sometimes provide subtle information to address this question (like whether their office hours are posted). Also consider contacting current and former students (more about this later in the chapter).

Postgraduate Careers

It may seem surprising, but many applicants don't look beyond graduate school to consider their ultimate careers. Getting into graduate school can seem like such an intense long-term hurdle that sometimes this step eclipses the ultimate career goal. Don't be distracted. Try to think ahead five to seven years to when you'll graduate. What happens then? Where do graduates go? Do they find jobs in academia, practice, or the "real world"? Some programs identify recent graduates and provide students with opportunities to contact them. Even if the graduate program that you're considering doesn't advertise such a service, the admissions office or department office may be able to put you in contact with a recent graduate. If you choose to speak with a recent graduate of the program, remember that he or she may report back to faculty, so be courteous and respectful.

Student Attrition

What is the program's attrition rate? Some programs accept only a small handful of students and then provide excellent academic, financial, and social support services to retain them. Other programs admit many more students than they can manage, offer little support, and lose many students or use difficult sequences of exams to actively weed out students. Try to find out how many students are admitted each year and how many drop out and graduate each year to infer the extent of emotional and tangible support you can expect as a student.

Time to Completion

How long does it take students to complete the degree program? In psychology, a two-year master's program and five- to seven-year Ph.D. program is common. If a doctoral program's average time to completion is close to seven years or beyond, you should examine it more closely to determine why. Are students matched to faculty members upon entry to the program or must they locate and attract faculty advisors on their own? If students must attract faculty members to supervise their research, are there support mechanisms to ensure that students don't fall through the cracks and end up with no supervision (and therefore no degree)?

Campus Facilities and Resources

Are there adequate computer facilities, labs, equipment, space, and other resources to conduct research? Is there money for travel to conferences? Are students provided with offices or shared space to study and interact? Are the classrooms, offices, and labs well-maintained and pleasant enough to endure throughout the program? Are there additional educational and reputation-related perks such as proximity to conferences, a professional journal, or opportunities to become published in your field?

Financial Support

We'll discuss the various forms of financial support available in Chapter 3, but for now, consider the forms of financial support described on the application materials and program website. Are research and teaching assistantships available to fund students? Are scholarships and other sources of support available? What are the tuition and fees? Although cost is important to consider, don't rule out any programs on the basis of cost alone. Most graduate programs offer financial support to students they want to attract and there are a multitude of resources for obtaining additional support, so do not omit any programs for financial reasons.

Prestige

Should you worry about the prestige of the university or program to which you're applying? Perhaps. Whether prestige matters depends on what you hope to do with your degree (i.e., if you hope to enter the ivory tower). In academia, departmental prestige is loosely related to job quality (Peters, 1992). Doctoral recipients from prestigious departments are more likely to land prestigious jobs (e.g., at research institutions with small teaching loads that enable time for research and publication) than are those from less distinguished institutions. In academia, your teaching load in your first job often predicts your career because professors carrying heavy teaching loads have little time for the research and publication that is needed to advance to more prestigious institutions. The other benefit of attending a prestigious department is networking; advisors and mentors in such departments tend to have excellent reputations and connections that can help you advance in your career. However, if you are planning on a career as a practitioner, then prestige is less important because graduates of less prestigious institutions gain licensure and practice therapy with little difficulty. Similarly, prestige is less important at the master's degree level because most master's-level psychologists are involved in applied activities.

Geography

Gaining admission to graduate school in psychology is very difficult—you know this by now, but it's so difficult that many experts advise that applicants should not include geographic location as a criteria for evaluating or eliminating potential programs. With that in mind, I advise that you *should* consider geographic location, *if* it would significantly influence your happiness. Graduate school is a lengthy process, so you should consider a geographic move carefully but try not to rule out programs based on geography alone. Ask yourself

- Can I live here for several years?
- Can I handle the political and social climate?
- Would I be happier in a small town or a large urban area?
- Does the area offer the cultural and recreational activities that I need?
- What kind of impact will this location have on my family and friends?
- If you have a spouse, consider the employment opportunities in the area, as well.

Whether to move far away to attend graduate school is a difficult decision that requires that you carefully consider your career goals. Don't shy away from moving simply because it's scary or because you're afraid of being lonely. This is your future that you're playing with—is it worth a few years of potentially minor discomfort? You also might be pleasantly surprised by a move and come to love your new home.

MAKING CONTACT

Should you visit the campus or make contact with faculty or current students before you submit an application? Do you have significant questions about a particular program? Can you afford a trip to a school that you ultimately may not attend? Certainly nothing can give you a better perspective on a potential program than a campus visit. If you visit the campus you'll be able to observe faculty and student interactions, get a glimpse at the accessibility of faculty, perhaps sit in on a class, and determine if the campus and community satisfy your lifestyle and extracurricular needs.

If you're considering visiting the campus, do so before you submit your application. After you've submitted your application, you're officially an applicant and the faculty and admissions committee will be concerned about fairness to other applicants and so may not meet with you. Be sure to contact the admissions office and department as you plan your trip to set up appointments to visit faculty whose work interests you.

Also remember that a campus visit isn't necessary at this stage in the applications process. If you advance, you may visit the campus for an interview, and if you're accepted you can certainly visit before making your decision. So if funds are tight, you may want to wait on a campus visit rather than possibly waste time and money.

If the purpose of considering a visit is to meet students, faculty, and staff, you can establish limited contact and get some questions answered through phone conversations and email. Before asking questions about the program, reread all of the application materials that you've received to ensure that you haven't overlooked the answer. If you're certain that the materials don't address your question, then contact the admissions office. Try to place all of your questions into as few email messages or phone calls as possible. Admissions offices tend to be inundated with applicant questions, most of which already are answered in the admissions materials. When an applicant asks a question that's answered in the admissions materials, staff at the admissions office simply assume that the applicant didn't read the materials carefully—which is not the image you want to project, so be careful when asking questions about the program.

If you'd like to meet a current student to learn about their perspective on the graduate program, contact the admissions office and ask for contact information for a current student who is willing to talk about the program (sometimes this information is listed on department web pages). You'll probably get an email address and can send the student a message. Compose your message carefully with a few specific questions and ask if it's possible to talk by phone. Remember that students are busy so don't make a pest of yourself, but ask a few meaningful questions. If possible, try to talk on the phone for a few minutes because subtleties are more likely to come through in a conversation over the phone than by email. Be polite and remember that the student may report the conversation back to his or her advisor—the "walls," so to speak, have ears!

Remember that it's generally best to only contact faculty whose research interests you if you have an intelligent question to ask about their work. Faculty are busy and you're better off having more limited contact with them at this point in the admissions process; however, if you're truly interested in their work and have done your homework and can carry on a conversation about it, then feel free to send a short email explaining your interest in the program and the faculty member's work, and asking for preprints (copies of articles that are in press and have not yet been published).

If you make contact with a program, whether through a visit, email, or phone call, take notes and place your notes in the designated program's file so that you can use them in preparing your application and making decisions. Remembering what you've learned from contacting the program may seem like a simple task, but if you're applying to several programs, it's easy to confuse them and forget important information.

It's your job to choose the programs to which you'll apply. Don't simply hope to be accepted by any program—this is your future, after all. Throughout this chapter we've discussed the many considerations entailed in choosing a graduate school. For another perspective, read the tips from graduate students in Exhibit 1. While it may seem time intensive and overwhelming, putting in effort before sending applications can save you time and money in the long run. Did you know that most programs charge a $40 to $60 application fee? It makes financial sense—and of course educational sense—to apply only to those programs in which you're interested. Use the tools in this chapter to weed out the programs that don't meet your needs, and apply only to those programs that will prepare you for the career you ultimately desire.

Exhibit 1. Tips from Graduate Students

- Do some soul searching on what you'd like to do on a day-to-day and week-to-week basis for the next ten years. Also do some research on the employment conditions and salary projections for the next decade. Will your expensive degree be worth it? Talk to current professionals and get their input too.
- Look at all of your options and don't simply settle for the first school that accepts you. Take a long hard look at the school and decide if it will make you happy. If you're not happy with where you are, your graduate school years won't be as fantastic as they should be.
- As you consider schools, evaluate which school has the best to offer–not which one your friend is attending.
- I wish I had done my own grad school search differently. I'd look at the *APA Monitor* and study the jobs that interest me, noting what credentials are sought after.
- Do some "backwards thinking." Think about what you want to DO with a degree in psychology. Then consider what kinds of training you need to be successful in that career. Then look for programs and schools that offer that particular type of training.
- Read journal articles and book chapters that match your research interests. Write down the authors who do work similar to your interests and then look up where they teach (the Internet is great for this kind of research; just type their name into Google.com). Email those authors to see if they are accepting graduate students and introduce yourself and your background and interests. Also ask your professors for names of faculty at graduate programs who they think match your interests.
- Talk to students who are enrolled in the graduate programs you're interested in. Don't just trust the info you find on websites and brochures as it can be out of date or simply inaccurate.

Chapter 3

PREPARING FOR GRADUATE SCHOOL: IMPROVING YOUR CREDENTIALS

Did you know that admission to graduate school in some areas of psychology is more competitive than getting into medical school? Only about seven of every 100 applicants gain entry to doctoral programs in psychology (with about 4% of applicants admitted into clinical or counseling doctoral programs and 10% admitted into doctoral programs in other areas of psychology; Keith-Spiegel, Tabachnick, & Spiegel, 1994). Admissions committees receive hundreds of applications to fill a handful of slots, so committee members look for reasons to exclude applicants. For example, some departments use cutoff GPA and GRE scores to weed out less prepared applicants. If you don't score above the cutoff point, your file is removed from the stacks of application files (regardless of your research experience or stellar letters of recommendation)–and the admissions committee's task becomes a little bit easier. Competition is stiff, so it's essential that you understand what graduate admissions committees are looking for and work to improve your credentials and fulfill their expectations so that you don't end up in the slush pile.

WHAT DO ADMISSIONS COMMITTEES LOOK FOR?

So just what do admissions committees look for? They attempt to identify applicants who will become important researchers and leaders in their field. In other words, admissions committees try to select the most promising students. But what's a promising student? One who promises to be an excellent graduate student. The ideal graduate student is gifted, eager to learn, and highly motivated. He or she can work independently and take direction, supervision, and constructive criticism without becoming upset or overly sensitive. Faculty look for students who are hard workers, desire to work closely with faculty, are responsible and easy to work with, and who are a good fit to the program. The best graduate students complete the program on time, with distinction, and excel in the professional world to make program faculty proud. Of course, these are *ideals.* Most graduate students have some of these characteristics, but nearly no one will have all, so don't fear.

Now that you know the ideal to which graduate faculty strive in selecting new graduate students, let's look at how faculty weigh the various criteria for admission. Unfortunately there is no simple answer; each graduate admissions committee is a bit different, but generally speaking, the following criteria are important to most admissions committees:

- Undergraduate grade point average (especially the last two years of college)
- Graduate Record Exam (GRE) scores
- Recommendation letters
- Personal statement

Sure, you knew these things were important, but let's talk more about why and the part they play in admissions decisions.

GPA and GRE Scores

Grades are important not as a sign of intelligence, but instead as a long term indicator how well you perform your job as student. They reflect your motivation and your ability to do consistently good or bad work. Not all grades are the same, though. Admissions committees understand that applicants' grade point averages often cannot be compared meaningfully. Grades can differ among universities–an A at one university may be a B+ at another. Also grades differ among professors in the same university. Admissions committees try to take these things into account when examining applicants' GPAs. They also look at the courses taken: a B in Advanced Statistics may be worth more than an A in Introduction to Social Problems. In other words, they consider the context of the GPA: where was it obtained and of what courses is it comprised? In many cases, it's better to have a lower GPA composed of solid challenging courses than a high GPA based on easy courses like "Basket Weaving for Beginners" and the like.

Clearly, applicants' grade point averages are difficult to compare. This is where Graduate Record Exam (GRE) scores come in. Whereas grade point averages are not standardized (there are enormous differences in how professors within a department, university, or country grade student work), the GRE is. Your GRE score provides information about how you rank among your peers (that's why it's important to do your best! More on this in Chapter 5). Although GRE scores are standardized, departments don't weigh them in a standardized way. How a department or admissions committee evaluates GRE scores varies—some use them as cutoffs to eliminate applicants, some use them as criteria for research assistantships and other forms of funding, some look to GRE scores to offset weak GPAs, and some admissions committees will overlook poor GRE scores if applicants demonstrate significant strengths in other areas.

Letters of Recommendation

Usually admissions committees begin the evaluation process by considering grades (especially in the last 2 years of undergraduate study) and standardized test scores (i.e., GRE scores). These quantitative measures only tell a small part of an applicant's story. Letters of recommendation provide context within which to consider an applicant's numerical scores. Therefore it's important that the faculty who write your letters of recommendation know you well so that they can discuss the person behind the GPA and GRE scores. Generally speaking, letters written by professors known to committee members tend to carry more weight than those written by "unknowns." Letters written by well-known people in the field, if they signify that they know you well and think highly of you, can be very helpful in moving your application towards the top of the list. We'll talk more about recommendation letters and how to get them later in this book.

Personal Statement

The personal statement, also known as the admissions essay, statement of purpose, and personal goal statement, is your chance to introduce yourself, speak directly to the admissions committee, and provide information that doesn't appear elsewhere in your application. Faculty read personal statements very closely because they reveal lots of information about applicants. Your essay is an indicator of your writing ability, motivation, ability to express yourself, maturity, passion for the field, and judgment. Admissions committees read essays with the intent to learn more about applicants, to determine if they have the qualities and attitudes needed for success, and to weed out applicants who don't fit the program. An excellent essay can boost an applicant with mediocre GPA and GRE scores, and a poor essay can send applicants with high scores walking. In Chapter 6, we'll talk more about the admissions essay and provide concrete advice to help you present yourself in the best possible light.

Faculty Perspectives

In addition to the various parts of your application, recognize that another element plays into the admissions puzzle: Faculty interests. Faculty members have their own incentives for choosing students–beyond objective criteria like GPAs and GRE scores. Faculty members look for potential colleagues. They try to choose students who are or will become capable researchers and teachers who can assist them with their work and ease the burden of the professorate.

Graduate departments are diverse and must represent all areas of psychology, so it's likely that only one or two faculty are hired from each subfield of psychology. Professors can sometimes feel isolated because they may not have a departmental colleague who knows about or is interested in their research area. Faculty members search for students whose interests match their own so that they will have an interested and competent junior colleague to assist them in furthering their research. Of course, accepting a student with similar interests isn't just a faculty member's way of reducing boredom or isolation; it's essential for his or her career advancement. Professors are evaluated on the basis of their research productivity–publications in scholarly journals. Raises, promotions, and incentives are allocated to professors on the basis of research productivity, so professors seek competent graduate students to assist them in increasing their research output and enhancing their scholarly work (Keith-Spiegel & Wiederman, 2000).

In addition to selecting students whose research interests match their own, faculty members look for students who are competent and won't need excess guidance. Students who know what they want to do and why they're attending graduate school and who have defined, but flexible, research interests are sought after. Faculty members also look for students who are easy to work with, personality-wise. Students who have pleasant personalities, can handle criticism, and are honest are easy to mentor. Essentially, professors look for students who make their jobs easier—who contribute to their teaching and research, are competent, and are easy to get along with.

Secondary Admissions Criteria

By now I'm sure that you're aware that admissions committees are faced with many more qualified applicants than they can admit. That's when secondary criteria come into play to determine who stands out. Secondary criteria that committees consider first are (Bonifazi, Crespy, & Rieker, 1997; Keith-Spiegel, Tabachnick, & Spiegel, 1994):

- match between the applicant's skills and interests and the program goals
- research experience resulting in a paper presentation at a professional conference or publication in a scholarly journal
- experience as a research assistant
- degree to which the applicant is knowledgeable about and interested in the program
- Number of research methodology and statistics courses taken
- Number of science (e.g., biology, chemistry, physics) courses taken
- Prestige of the applicant's undergraduate psychology department (i.e., faculty research productivity and status)
- Prestige of applicant's undergraduate institution
- Potential for success revealed in an interview or other form of personal contact
- Honors or merit scholarships awarded to the applicant

How can this information help you in preparing your applications? Three things are apparent. First, research experience is very important to admissions committees. Second, committees look for students who match their programs, so take the time to research programs and tailor your application materials to each program. Finally, take courses that demonstrate your ability to think analytically and your preparedness for graduate study. Take additional courses in research, statistics, science, and math.

HOW CAN YOU IMPROVE YOUR CREDENTIALS?

Now that you have an overview of what graduate admissions committees consider in reviewing applications, let's talk about how to improve your credentials for admission to the graduate program of your choice. Note that other chapters in this book examine the GRE, personal statement, and recommendation letters in depth, so here we focus on improving your credentials through coursework, and the last section of this chapter discusses the importance of obtaining practical experience (e.g., research and field experience).

Your GPA

What grades should you strive for? What, exactly, are "good" grades? The average minimum GPA that most programs will consider is 3.2 for doctoral programs and 3.0 for master's programs (American Psychological Association, 1997). Generally speaking, with a 3.4 GPA you can expect to be admitted to some Psy.D. or Ph.D. programs (assuming that you meet all of the other criteria). Recognize that many programs don't use cutoffs but examine each applicant's admission packet as a whole. In other words, they evaluate GPA within the context of the other elements including GRE scores, letters of recommendation, personal statements, and relevant experience.

If your GPA isn't as high as you'd like, don't fear. Break your GPA down. Did you perform better in your junior and senior years of college than in your freshman and sophomore years? Admissions committees are interested in your recent performance, so higher grades in your last two years of college can offset mediocre grades during your first two years. What's your GPA for your major? Did you perform better in your psychology classes than in other classes? That helps. What courses compose your transcript? Did you take lots of challenging science and math courses? If so, then remember that admissions committees will take the level of difficulty into account when considering your GPA.

Preferred Coursework

So what courses do graduate admissions committees look for?

- Statistics
- Psychology of Learning
- Experimental Psychology
- Developmental Psychology
- Physiological Psychology
- Abnormal Psychology
- Research Methodology
- Cognitive Psychology
- Sensation and Perception

In addition to psychology coursework, graduate admissions committees are interested in students who have a broad educational background in the spirit of a liberal arts education. In other words, don't take every psychology course offered in your undergraduate course catalogue. Graduate programs look for generalists, not specialists. They seek well-rounded students. So, take courses in a range of disciplines and be sure to take extra courses in science and math to demonstrate your ability to think analytically. Consider courses in:

- Biology
- Chemistry
- Math
- English
- Philosophy
- Computer Science
- Anthropology

Many applicants to psychology graduate programs wonder if majoring in psychology is necessary to gain admission to a graduate program in psychology. In short, the answer is, "No." You don't have to major in psychology to win admission to psychology graduate programs (even doctoral programs!). That said, however, recognize that you should have taken the psychology, methodology, and statistics courses listed above to demonstrate that you know what you're getting into (i.e., that you understand the scope of psychology) and you're capable of handling psychology coursework.

Can You Raise Your GPA?

If you're in your sophomore or junior years of college, begin a campaign to improve your grades immediately. Some students try to improve their GPAs by taking easy courses. Don't take this route to a higher GPA because admissions committees carefully examine applicant transcripts, so your reliance on good grades in fluffy courses to improve your GPA will be quickly revealed. It won't be viewed favorably, either, because easy courses are easy for everyone, so succeeding doesn't demonstrate your ability as a serious scholar. This doesn't mean that you should shy away from easy courses, just don't overload on them in an attempt to improve your GPA. Instead, take courses that will demonstrate your scholarly competence, even if it means that your GPA will be a little lower.

One of the best ways to raise your GPA is by becoming a more disciplined student. Set up a schedule to ensure that you set aside the needed time to study. Set aside about one and one-half hours to two hours of study time for each hour in class. If you're taking five 3-credit classes, you should spend a minimum of 15 to 20 hours studying each week. How do you find the time? That's where a schedule comes in handy. Begin by picking up an organizer, or creating a table that lists each hour of the day and each day of the week. Write in all of your time commitments (e.g., times that classes meet, regular appointments, working hours, etc.). Then, take a look at all of the empty space–these are the slots from which you'll choose study periods. Think about when you're at your best. When is it easiest to concentrate and focus on academic tasks? Some people are at their best in the mornings, others at night, and others have several windows throughout the day in which they are most efficient. Choose your study times with an eye towards maximizing your efficiency, so pick times to study that you're at your best. Also remember to leave 15- to 20-minute breaks every two hours or so to clear your head and freshen your thoughts. Also make sure to schedule flexible time for fun and friends. The benefit of a schedule is that you'll be able to set aside time for work and for play.

In addition to scheduling time to study, successful students set aside special places to study. Choose a place that's easily accessible to you and where you can concentrate. Have a place where all you do is study. Soon you'll find that your mind gets into studying mode when you enter your special study space, whether it's your desk, a corner of the library, or a quiet room at home. Your study space should be:

- well lit. Good lighting makes reading easier on the eyes and keeps you from getting tired.
- quiet. Study in a place that's out of the way of distractions.
- comfortable. Choose a comfortable and sturdy chair.
- organized. Make sure that you have enough open space to spread out and have all of your books, notes, and other study materials handy so that you don't waste valuable study time looking for your stuff.

Getting good grades entails more than scheduling study time and setting up a study space, but setting aside a time and place for studying is a large part of the battle for better grades. For more tips on studying, check out my book, *The Psychology Major's Handbook* (2003), which explains in detail how to take notes in class, study, take tests, and write papers.

What If It's Too Late?

If you're a senior in college or have already graduated, there are still steps you can take to improve your credentials. Consider retaking courses in which you scored poorly. Some colleges average the two grades, whereas others don't. Even if your GPA doesn't improve, the retaken course will show up on your transcript and it will demonstrate your initiative (only if you perform well, though!).

Other students delay graduation a year to take more coursework in math and science and get research experience (more on research experience later in this chapter). If you decide to go this route, take only those courses you can handle because mediocre performance won't help your case. Focus on courses that are regarded highly by psychology graduate programs (see the list provided earlier in this chapter). Even if you've already graduated, taking additional courses can show your motivation and dedication.

PRACTICAL EXPERIENCE AND YOUR GRADUATE APPLICATION

Applying to graduate school is very much like applying for a job in that relevant experience is very helpful in demonstrating your fit to the program and winning acceptance. Gain practical experience to demonstrate your interest and passion for the field, as well as to be sure that graduate study is for you. Graduate admissions committees look favorably on applicants with practical experience because such experiences show that you know what's involved in your chosen career and are competent in performing the kind of work that's required. Depending on your graduate school aspirations, seek practical experiences in research or practice settings.

Research Experience

Graduate programs in psychology, especially Ph.D. programs, highly value research experience. Without such experience, it's unlikely that even applicants with straight A's will gain admission to graduate programs in psychology. To make the short list of acceptances, you must demonstrate that you're capable of working to extend the field by generating new knowledge through the conduct of research. Gain research experience as an undergraduate student and admissions committees will be more confident that you understand what research is all about and have the ability (and motivation) to do it.

How to Get Involved in Research

In short, you must seek opportunities to get involved in research. How? First, excel in your courses and take time to get to know faculty (e.g., stop by their office hours to ask intelligent questions). Faculty look for students who are motivated, bright, and personable, so if you do well in class and are generally pleasant, they might approach you to ask if you're interested in helping out with some research. Of course, don't wait to be asked to get involved in research, take the initiative. Talk with faculty and let them know that you're interested in obtaining research experience. Ask if they need any help with projects or know someone who is looking for a volunteer to assist with research. Think back to classes that you've taken. Do any professors stand out? Did any talk about the research that they conduct? Perhaps a professor in your department has published an interesting article. Remember, that although having taken a class with the professor may help to break the ice, you should also approach professors whose work interests you, regardless of whether you've taken their classes.

If you find a professor with whom you might like to work, read a couple of his or her articles. This preliminary background reading will show the professor that you're serious, interested in assisting him or her, and motivated. Send the professor your resume and a cover letter mentioning the articles you've read and why his or her work interests you. Express your interest in assisting with the work and include information such as your grade point average and the courses that you've taken. Ask to set up an appointment. When you meet with the professor, express your interest, and ask whether you may assist him or her. Most professors are glad to have an extra pair of hands to work on their research projects, but sometimes professors are overwhelmed with students who wish to assist them. If the professor doesn't need additional assistance, ask if he or she knows whether other professors are looking for research assistants.

What's in It for You?

Understand that, in all likelihood, your work will be unpaid. What do you get in return? Experience. You'll get to see what research is all about and get a taste as to whether it's for you. Sometimes students initially have lukewarm interests in research–they get involved because it will look good on their application to graduate school. But once they see what it's like to make new discoveries, they become enthralled with the process and realize that research is fascinating. In addition to broadening your perspective on research, students often can obtain academic credit for their work as research assistants. If you're heavily involved in the project and it's successful, you may receive an acknowledgment in a journal article, a presentation at a professional conference, or perhaps even coauthorship on a journal article. An added benefit of working closely with a faculty member on his or her research is that the faculty member will get to know you well and can write a letter of recommendation that describes your potential for succeeding in graduate school. By working with you over time, he or she will be able to describe your skills and strengths in a much more detailed way than if you were simply a student in class.

What If Professors Aren't Doing Interesting Research?

Remember that your research experience doesn't have to be in your area of interest. Any research experience will help. Besides, sometimes it's good to get involved in different areas of research because you may discover new interests. As an undergraduate, a variety of broad experiences that provide you with a taste of several research areas is better than conducting research only in your area of interest. Of course, if you're completely disinterested in the research topic it might be difficult to remain motivated and do a good job. Understand your interest level and limits when deciding whether to assist a faculty member with his or her research because poor or inconsistent work will not be helpful and can hurt your chances for a persuasive letter of recommendation that benefits your application to graduate school. Regardless of the research topic, many of the tasks that research assistants complete can be tedious: copying, sharpening pencils, administering surveys, entering data into SPSS, and so on. Sure, some of these tasks are boring, but they're necessary for completing the research project.

Be a Responsible Research Assistant

If you get involved in research remember that the faculty member is depending on you. He or she can't afford to have assistants who are unreliable or careless. Agreeing to assist a faculty member with his or her research is a big commitment that you shouldn't take lightly. Your research tasks should come first–treat the research project as a class and be diligent. There's nothing worse than a student who is enthusiastic at first but disappears or performs inconsistent and careless work. The research project gets disrupted, tasks often must be completed again, and the faculty member loses faith in the student. If you find yourself in such a situation, you won't be able to ask the faculty member for a letter of recommendation. Also understand that faculty talk–other professors may learn about the quality of your work which can influence your interactions with them as well. In other words, if you're going to assist a professor with his or her research, be responsible or you may not like the consequences.

Field Experience

If you plan on a career as a practicing psychologist, seek field experiences that will allow you to gain experience in practice settings. Such experience will help you to see if working with clients is really for you, and if that's what you want to do throughout your career. Similar to research experience when applying to research-oriented (e.g., Ph.D.) programs, admissions committees for practitioner-oriented programs look for applicants who have clinical or community service experience. Generally, only seek service experience if you're applying to a practice-oriented clinical, counseling, or school psychology program. While service experience will not hurt your application to research oriented programs, it will provide little advantage and will detract from your time for gaining the more important research experience.

How do you get field experience? Many psychology departments offer service-learning classes in which students complete clinical or community service requirements in addition to their coursework. For example, my own department offers a course in Community Psychology, in which students complete five hours per week of service within a community, clinical, or social service agency in addition to attending class. You can learn about other opportunities for field experience in the community from your advisor. Try to gain experience in the area in which you hope to concentrate. So, if you're interested in clinical and counseling programs, seek experience in a mental health or human services setting under the supervision of a psychologist or other licensed mental health professional (e.g., psychiatrist, counselor, or social worker). The benefits of field experience are that you get applied experience. For example, at a field placement at a local social service agency you might assist in the intake of clients, assessment and reporting, as well as behavioral modification. You'll have the chance to see what it's like to work in an applied setting (which is really important if you're considering becoming a practitioner) and gain new knowledge and skills that you can't learn in a classroom setting.

No matter what, start searching for field experience opportunities early, in your sophomore or junior year. Many students wait until late in their junior or senior years of college and don't realize that it takes time to set up such an experience. Also, you'll need time after beginning your field experience to learn the ropes and demonstrate your competence. A letter of recommendation from a faculty member who's supervised your fieldwork or your supervisor at your placement will enhance your application to practice-oriented programs because it will be clear that you understand what you're getting into and have the skills to work with and help people.

Exhibit 2. Tips from Graduate Students

- Begin doing research early in your undergraduate years and do as much as possible.
- Seek practical experience. Obviously you can't see clients, but there are other opportunities like working at a camp for children with particular needs.
- Contact professors and offer to help in their labs.
- Work closely with faculty or graduate students on research so that you'll have opportunities to present at conferences.
- Take extra statistics and research courses.
- Plan early to be sure that you have enough time to get the experiences you need to be competitive.
- Become a research assistant for a professor, even if you're unpaid. Try to make the most of it, even if it's just data entry. Ask questions and find some personal interest and relevance in the research.
- If you're looking into clinical programs, volunteer in clinical settings like hospitals, day treatment programs, residential facilities, suicide hotlines etc.
- Develop good study skills early in college.

Chapter 4

OVERVIEW OF THE APPLICATION PROCESS

You've already had a taste of what applying to graduate school entails, but you should understand that it's hard to make broad statements about the graduate admissions process because schools and departments differ with regard to how they manage the admissions process. Recognize that some schools to which you apply may do things differently. It's your job to learn about any differences.

COMPONENTS OF THE APPLICATION

So what does a graduate application entail? Your application packet is comprised of many pieces: application forms, personal statement, curriculum vitae, standardized test scores, official transcript, and three letters of recommendation from faculty.

Application Forms

You'll find that each school has its own set of application forms, usually for both the university and department. Carefully review these forms and understand that, although it may seem unreasonable, neatness counts when it comes to completing graduate school applications. Must you handwrite each form? No. Use a scanner to scan the forms into the computer–and then you can neatly type your application and print it out. Of course, if you're applying to many schools, scanning and typing becomes tedious very quickly.

Many universities offer applicants the option of completing their applications on the Web, which saves time waiting for schools to mail you their application forms and wondering whether your forms have been received (or lost in the snail mail vacuum!). If you choose to submit your graduate applications online, create a word processing file with all of your vital information. Spell check and proofread your application and then cut and paste from the word processing file to the application form. Perhaps the most difficult part of online applications is searching the Web for each school, and then searching each school's Web page for the application form itself. Most applications will require you to create a username and password so that you can save your work and reenter to complete your application over several sittings. Be sure to save your username, password, and the Internet address for the entry page. Also, beware because some programs have a broad universitywide application online, while the specific graduate program has a written form. Some students find it easier to keep track of the multiple requirements and requirements for submitting applications on a spreadsheet.

For an easy alternative, try a commercial application service that can handle all of your applications at once. You complete one form, and your vital information is added to each application automatically. Attach whatever essays are needed for each school. Enter your credit card number to pay each school's application fees, and with relatively few clicks, you're done. PrincetonReview.com (at http://www.princetonreview.com) allows you to apply to over 700 graduate schools online with a minimum of fuss.

Personal Statement

The personal statement, also known as admissions essay, statement of purpose, and personal goal statement, is a short writing sample that introduces you to the admissions committee and provides information that doesn't appear elsewhere in your application. It's a chance for the admissions committee to see you as a person behind the numbers. In your personal statement, you'll describe your qualifications and explain why you're interested in the program. Describe your college experiences, research experience, and volunteer projects that contribute to your career and professional development and goals. Admissions committees will examine your personal statement to get an understanding of who you are but also to assess your writing skills, how well you communicate your ideas, and whether your interests fit the department/school to which you are applying. In Chapter 6 we examine the personal statement in detail.

Graduate Admissions Examination (GRE)

Students tend to dread the Graduate Admissions Exam, or the GRE. There are actually two GRE tests that you need to prepare for: the GRE General and the GRE Psychology test, both of which are standardized examinations that graduate admissions committees use to compare and evaluate applicants. The GRE General measures verbal, quantitative, and analytical abilities thought to predict likelihood of success in graduate school. Some (not all) programs also require applicants to take the GRE Subject Test in Psychology, which measures your general knowledge of psychological concepts. Many students believe that it is impossible to study for these exams, but that's not true. For example, if you haven't taken a mathematics course in some time, review the quantitative skills tested by the GRE. Study for the psychology subtest by reviewing a comprehensive textbook for introductory psychology. For more information about the GRE and how you can prepare, see Chapter 5.

Transcripts

Your application is not complete until the institution receives your official transcript from your undergraduate institution. An official transcript is sent directly by your undergraduate college or university to the school(s) to which you're applying and bears the college seal. If you attended more than one institution, you will need to request an official transcript from each institution you attended. In examining your transcript, admissions committees will consider the following:

- your overall GPA
- quality of the undergraduate institution
- your grades in your major subject area and particularly in the upper division courses and within the past two years
- patterns of improvement if you did not have a strong start

Remember to request your transcripts from the registrar's office early because most offices take a few days or even a week to process your request. Also understand that if you wait until the end of the fall semester to request transcripts they may be delayed as most offices close for the holidays (sometimes taking an extended break). Save yourself grief: Request transcripts early. Also, include a copy of your unofficial transcript with your application and a note that the official transcript has been requested so that admissions committees have something to review until the official copy arrives.

Letters of Recommendation

Most students don't realize until it's too late that they will need three letters of recommendation to apply to graduate school. Letters of recommendation are usually obtained from faculty and sometimes other professionals in a position to provide an evaluation of your academic and professional strengths and weaknesses (e.g., a supervisor at a practicum or other field experience site). Admissions committees read letters of recommendation to learn about your capacity for fulfilling academic requirements and working with others. An effective letter of recommendation presents a balanced perception of your skills and abilities and demonstrates that your referee knows you well. The most helpful letters come from professors who have had lots of contact with you. Letters that simply restate your coursework aren't helpful because they duplicate information available on your transcript; instead, such letters tell the reader that you haven't had sufficient contact with faculty outside of the classroom (e.g., in research or applied settings). The admissions committee might assume that you're not assertive, but simply fade into the background in a classroom setting, say nothing in class, and perform well on tests, for example. To get a great letter, you must develop relationships with faculty, which means that you must get involved outside of the classroom, in research, in *Psi Chi* and other psychology-related activities. In Chapter 7 we talk about how to form relationships with faculty and request letters of recommendation. Also see Chapter 3 for information about the value of obtaining research experience and how to do so.

Curriculum Vitae

This isn't a formal component of a graduate application. In fact, most schools don't ask for a curriculum vitae or CV. What's a CV? A curriculum vitae or CV is an academic resume that highlights your scholarly accomplishments. Although most students compose a CV while in graduate school, consider including one in your application. A CV is not a formal part of your graduate application and few schools request it. A CV provides the admissions committee with a clear outline of your accomplishments so they can determine whether you're a good fit with their program. When it is properly prepared, a CV demonstrates that you are scholarly and familiar with the workings of an academic setting. Begin your curriculum vitae early and revise it as you progress towards (and through!) graduate school and you can easily chart your accomplishments and impress a graduate admissions committee.

Unlike a resume, which is one to two pages in length, a curriculum vitae grows in length throughout your academic career. What goes into a CV? Here are the types of information that a curriculum vitae may contain. Your vitae probably will not have all of these sections yet, but at least consider each.

- *Contact Information.* Here, include your name, address, phone, fax, and email for home and office, if applicable. If you are currently in school and have two addresses, remember to distinguish between your current and permanent address. Also include the phone number and email address where you can most easily be reached. If you have a professional looking web page, you can include that as well, but if your web page is of a personal nature and not related to your ultimate career goals, leave it out.
- *Education.* Indicate your major, type of degree, and the date each degree was awarded for each postsecondary school attended. Eventually you'll include titles of theses or dissertations and chairs of committees. If you haven't yet completed your degree, indicate the expected graduation date. In regard to the education section, list degrees as "anticipated" if they have not yet been awarded. If you have an outstanding grade point average, you may include it in this section.
- *Honors and Awards.* List each award, granting institution, and the date awarded. If you have only one award (e.g., graduation honors), consider incorporating this information within the education section.
- *Teaching Experience.* List any courses that you assisted with as a TA, co-taught, or taught. Note the institution, role held in each, and

supervisor. This section will become more relevant during your graduate school years, but sometimes undergraduates are assigned teaching roles.

- *Research Experience.* List assistantships, practica, and other research experience. Include the institution, nature of the position, duties, dates, and supervisor.
- *Statistical and Computer Experience.* This section is especially relevant for research-oriented doctoral programs. List courses that you've taken, statistical and computer programs with which you're familiar, and data analysis techniques with which you're competent.
- *Professional Experience.* List relevant professional experience such as administrative work and summer jobs.
- *Grants Awarded.* Include title of agency, projects for which funds were awarded, and dollar amounts.
- *Publications.* You'll probably begin this section during graduate school. Eventually you'll separate publications into sections for articles, chapters, reports, and other documents. Document each publication in APA style.
- *Conference Presentations.* Similar to the section on publications, separate this category into sections for posters and papers. Document each presentation in APA style. Document each presentation in APA publication style.
- *Professional Activities.* List service activities, committee memberships, administrative work, lectures you've been invited to deliver, professional workshops you've delivered or attended, editorial activities, and any other professional activities in which you've engaged.
- *Professional Affiliations.* List any professional societies with which you're affiliated (e.g., student affiliate of the American Psychological Association, or the American Psychological Society).
- *Research Interests.* Briefly summarize your research interests with four to six key descriptors. Remember that you're not wedded to these areas, but it gives the admissions committee an idea of your interests and shows that you've thought about the research that you'd like to conduct.
- *Teaching Interests.* List courses you're prepared to teach or would like the opportunity to teach. You probably won't include this section in your CV until the end of graduate school.

- *References.* Provide names, phone numbers, addresses, and email addresses for your referees. Ask their permission beforehand. Be sure that they will speak highly of you.

Present items chronologically within each category of the CV, with the most recent items first. Your curriculum vitae is a statement of your accomplishments, and most importantly, is a work in progress. Update it frequently and you'll find that taking pride in your accomplishments can be source of motivation. Exhibit 3 presents a sample curriculum vitae.

Overall Presentation

Don't worry, you don't have to prepare a presentation! But presentation counts in the graduate admissions process. What do I mean by presentation? How you present your application materials reflects on you. Be sure that you present yourself in a professional manner. Type all parts of your application and any other formal communications that you send programs (e.g., follow-up letters). Be sure that your letters and personal statement and other writing is grammatically correct and that there are no spelling errors. Have someone else read everything to double check.

Be timely. Get your application in on time, if not early. It's your job to ensure that all application materials are in by the deadline. Many programs will not let you know if anything is missing from your application file so it's your obligation to check. Submit your application early so that you have time to ensure that all materials have been received by the application deadline. Never submit your application late. The members of the admissions committee will wonder if an applicant can't get an application in on time, how will he or she complete papers, class assignments, and research? Is it an indication of carelessness? Will he or she be generally tardy? If your application arrives early, you'll send the message that you're well organized and enthusiastic. Also, some members of the committee may begin reviewing applications before the deadline–early applications may get a more careful review before the application deluge hits.

Finally, stay organized. Make a copy of each complete application before you mail it, in case it gets lost in the mail or misfiled. Also keep track of all that you've done by making a checklist sheet for every program to which you're applying. List all that needs to be done and include your notes about your progress on each item. Send the application in a sturdy 9x11 envelope (don't fold any of the papers) and mail your application from the post office to ensure that it has the correct amount of postage. Some applicants choose to send their applications by priority mail so that they can track the packages and determine when they've arrived as well as who signed for them. Though this route is more expensive, it provides peace of mind.

Two to three weeks after you've mailed the application, call the admissions office or the department secretary (depending on where you sent the application) to ensure that it has reached them and is complete. Be calm and courteous because you don't know who you're speaking with and support staff are likely to tell faculty about applicants who are rude. Also remember that the support staff need time to organize applicant materials, so your materials may have arrived but may not have been filed yet (the office is likely to deal with over 100 and sometimes as many as 1,000 applications!).

PREPARING FOR GRADUATE ADMISSIONS: TIMETABLE

Now that you're familiar with what goes into the admissions packet, let's talk about what you need to do to round out your academic and professional background to prepare for graduate school admissions. Ideally you're reading this book in your freshman or sophomore year of college because many of the preparation tips provided below require time to implement (e.g., getting involved in research). However, even if you're in your junior or senior years you'll find advice to help you improve your credentials, so read on.

Sophomore Year

- Work on building a strong GPA. For tips on improving your GPA, see Chapter 3. If you need advice on studying and writing papers for your psychology courses, *The Psychology Major's Handbook* (2003) will walk you through the steps needed to refine your study habits and get better grades.
- Work on cultivating relationships with faculty. In your psychology classes, note your professors' research areas. Get in touch with

those professors whose research interests you, and talk with them about it.

- Take at least one more science and math course(s) beyond the requirements for your major and degree.
- If you're interested in clinical or counseling psychology, get some field experience in a clinically-relevant setting.
- Contact psychology professors who conduct research of interest to you and discuss the possibility of becoming involved. Try to develop a mentor relationship with a professor or two in your area of interest and follow their suggestions.
- Attend psychology-related seminars at your school and surrounding institutions, as well as local psychology conferences. Most departments post information about local and regional conferences and other opportunities for students on a departmental bulletin board or website. Ask students and faculty in your department where you can find such information. At psychology conventions, try to meet graduate students and find out what graduate school is like. Conventions are also a great place to learn about the latest research in psychology and meet faculty at institutions to which you might apply (remember to maintain a professional appearance and demeanor!).
- Attend graduate school informational meetings at your university. Most psychology departments host an informational meeting each year or even each semester. Attend as many as you can to gather tips and info about how to improve your credentials, prepare your application, and learn what graduate school is like.
- Join the Psychology Club at your university. It will enable you to get involved with other students and faculty who are interested in psychology and can lead to research and other educational opportunities. If your school doesn't have a psychology club, speak with a faculty member about starting one. If you choose to start a psychology club, remember that it will take a lot of time and hard work on your part but there's a big payoff. Don't give up. Your diligence in starting the club will help you to earn excellent recommendations from the faculty in your department–and will be a fantastic professional experience.
- Join the *Psi Chi* chapter at your school, if you meet the entry requirements. If not, work to meet the requirements.

Junior Year

- Continue taking additional math and science courses to strengthen your credentials and build a broad knowledge base of scientific skills.
- Continue cultivating relationships with faculty. Visit their office hours with intelligent questions.
- Get involved in research. Talk to faculty about assisting them with their research.
- Research areas of interest and begin thinking about the type of program to which you would like to apply.
- Research programs. Consult the APA publication, *Graduate Study in Psychology,* and follow the tips provided in Chapter 2 for locating graduate programs.
- Talk to your advisor about typical requirements for graduate admissions and seek advice on what you can do to strengthen your credentials.
- Prepare for the General GRE. Check out the GRE website at http://www.gre.org and become familiar with the various GRE subsections. Take a practice test and consider enrolling in a preparatory course. Take the GRE towards the end of your junior year so that you have time to retake it if needed.
- Prepare for the GRE Subject test in Psychology. Study the commercially available books and software and by rereading a good advanced general psychology textbook. Don't neglect the sections on statistics and methodology. Take the GRE Psychology test towards the end of your junior year or in the summer.
- Try to attend at least one professional conference in your field of study to get the "feel" of what goes on at these conferences. To learn about professional conferences, read the bulletin boards in your department or ask faculty about the annual meetings of regional psychological associations. Attending a professional conference is a great chance to develop a professional network with faculty and students at different schools.
- Continue your involvement in research and try to develop your own project to submit a paper to a conference (with the help of your faculty mentor).

- If you're interested in clinical or counseling psychology, get experience through volunteer work or a paid job. Try to do some research in connection with your volunteer activities.
- Investigate summer jobs or educational/research opportunities related to psychology. Many summer internships are available through laboratories or professional organizations. Check with your psychology department faculty on a regular basis concerning available opportunities and apply early.
- Meet with faculty and career counselors to discuss graduate programs and your plans for graduate school and beyond.
- Check your transcript for errors.

Summer Before Your Senior Year

- Request application materials, brochures, and financial aid forms from the schools to which you might apply. Chapter 2 offers tips for how to locate and select graduate programs.
- Visit institutions that interest you, if possible.
- If you haven't already taken the GRE, do so now.
- Consider which faculty members to ask for letters of recommendation.
- Create a timetable of application deadlines and plan your course of action for fall.
- Write a draft statement of purpose/personal statement.
- Prepare a curriculum vitae.
- Compile a preliminary list of programs that offer the area of concentration, degree, and training model that appeal to you.
- Obtain summer employment, experience, or education related to psychology.
- Retake in summer school any courses in which you received a grade below a "B" (especially statistics and research methods or experimental psychology).
- Calculate and save money for graduate school application fees (most institutions charge application fees in the $40 to $60 range), copying, and transcript costs.
- Verify your transcript. Get a copy of your transcript and check it carefully. Mistakes happen, and it's your responsibility to be sure that your transcript accurately reflects your academic history.

Senior Year, September

- Check with the registrar at your college and obtain a statement of your current standing to determine if you have any unmet academic requirements. You don't want any surprises next semester when you apply for graduation!
- If financial aid information was not included in the admissions materials that you've received, call the school's financial aid office. Ask for an informational packet, as well as any forms you will need to complete to be considered for financial aid.
- Note the deadlines for financial aid information to be submitted. Financial aid deadlines are often different than graduate admission deadlines and are sometimes much earlier than admissions deadlines.
- Request your recommendations as soon as possible. Some applications are due in December, so approach faculty well ahead of time to give faculty members plenty of time to respond and write letters that reflect well on you. Give your recommenders all the information that they will need to write recommendations for you (e.g., a copy of your transcript, each program's recommendation form, your statement of purpose, and information about each of the programs to which you're applying). Ask him or her if there's anything else that you can provide to help them (and see Chapter 7 for more information about letters of recommendation).
- Arrange for a conference with faculty who know about graduate schools in your preferred specialty area. Take them a copy of your resume and your list of preferred schools so that they can recommend schools for which you may qualify.
- If you didn't do as well as you expected on the GRE, or if you have not yet taken it, register for it now (try to take it no later than October). Remember that scores may take a month to reach the schools to which you're applying.
- Request transcripts early because during the latter part of fall quarter, the registrar gets backed up with many transcript requests. It's important to begin this process as early as possible, as the registrar's office may take weeks to process a request.
- Complete application forms. Make plenty of photocopies of each form and for best results, scan the forms into the computer.

- Ask faculty members to review your personal statement and curriculum vitae and provide feedback. Take their advice and revise your essays.

Senior Year, October

- Narrow down your list of schools to which you will apply. Check the application deadline for each school. Post these deadlines where you will see them everyday.
- Request that your GRE scores be sent to all schools to which you'll apply.
- Begin contacting individuals from whom you will request letters of recommendation.
- Get additional feedback on your personal statement and other essays that you'll prepare for specific programs.

Senior Year, November

- Request that your undergraduate transcript(s) be sent to all of the institutions to which you are applying. Keep in mind the deadline for each school.
- If you haven't yet requested letters of recommendation, do so now. Inform the person who is giving you the recommendation of the deadlines that are relevant. When handing in a request for a recommendation, always have a typed out description of your education, personal goals, long-range goals, etc.

Senior Year, December

- Carefully prepare final copies of all application materials (note that many applications are due in early January and sometimes late January/early February).
- Finalize your essays and statement of purpose. Don't forget to seek input from others. Spell check!
- Mail applications two to three weeks before they are due. It's a good idea to get your applications in early.
- Keep a photocopy of each application for your records.
- Make sure that your letters of recommendation are sent in.

- Apply for fellowships and other sources of financial aid, as applicable
- Relax and breathe!

Senior Year, January

- Some schools send a postcard upon receipt of each application. Keep track of these. If you don't receive a postcard or letter, contact the admissions office by email or phone to ensure that your application has been received before the deadline.
- Fill out the Federal Student Aid (FAFSA) application. You'll need your most recent tax forms to do this.

Senior Year, February

- Start planning for the admissions interviews. What questions will you ask? Prepare answers to common questions and review Chapter 9 for more information about interviews. Note that not all graduate programs conduct interviews, but if you're applying to a program in clinical or counseling psychology, expect an interview.

Senior Year, March/April

- Visit schools to which you've been accepted.
- Discuss acceptances and rejections with a faculty member.
- Notify the graduate program of your acceptance. Send a deposit to your institution of choice.
- Notify programs that you're declining, so they may admit students on their waiting list.
- Send thank-you notes to people who wrote your recommendation letters, informing them of your success.

FINANCIAL AID: HOW WILL I PAY FOR GRADUATE SCHOOL?

Exactly how are you going to pay for those extra years of education? A graduate degree can easily cost $50,000 and often more than $100,000. Plus, you'll need funding for more than just tuition. Since graduate school is a full-time job, you'll need money to cover your living expenses and all that income that you won't be earning as a graduate student. How do you pay for it all?

Requesting Aid

First, understand that financial aid applications are usually included in application packages. If it's not, call the financial aid office and request one. Your application may not automatically be considered for aid, so read the school catalog and application materials to learn about sources of funding and what forms or applications are required. Also note that most graduate school application packets have a place to check if you want to be considered for financial aid. Be sure to check those boxes!

After January 1, be sure to submit your FAFSA form. What's FAFSA? The U.S. Department of Education runs a variety of student financial assistance programs, but in order to qualify, your need for aid is assessed by the Free Application for Federal Student Aid (FAFSA) form. You can submit your FAFSA through snail mail or online at http://www.ed.gov/offices/OSFAP/Students/apply/express.html. Once you've submitted your FAFSA, you'll learn about your eligibility for these federally funded forms of aid:

- Federal Work-Study is essentially a part-time job that allows you to earn money for education-related expenses and get work experience on campus.
- Federal Perkins Loan is a low-interest loan for students with financial need. Perkins Loans don't begin accruing interest until nine months after you graduate.
- Stafford Loans and Supplemental Loans are additional loans available to graduate students. Stafford Loans don't begin accruing interest until six months after you graduate. Supplemental Loans do not defer interest; interest begins accruing during your graduate school years.

Submitting your FAFSA will also qualify you for scholarships and aid through your university, such as teaching and research assistantships, which can provide you with free tuition and an annual stipend between $6,000 and $15,000. Note that there are very few assistantships or institutional sources of financial support for master's students. Most assistantships are reserved for doctoral students who require more time to complete their degree programs and are viewed as apprentices more so than master's level students. For more suggestions on how to obtain funding for graduate school, see the tips from graduate students in exhibit 4.

Teaching Assistantship

Teaching assistantships require that you work part time, assisting a professor in teaching a class, teaching a lab or discussion section of a class, or sometimes teaching a class on your own. The benefits of a teaching assistantship including obtaining teaching experience, but also learning a field. You never learn a subject as well as when you teach it. Plus, you'll have the opportunity to interact closely with faculty members in your department, working with them closely, as colleagues of a sort, which can help you to establish yourself and become better known within the department and develop professional relationships that are critical to your future success.

An assistantship is no "free ride," of course. While the duties of a TA will vary, you can expect to be responsible for one or more of the following:

- assisting a professor with one or more sections of a course
- running laboratory or discussion sessions
- grading undergraduate student papers and exams
- holding regular office hours and meeting with students
- conducting study and review sessions
- teaching a course

On average, a TA is required to work about twenty hours per week, but if you're teaching your own sections of a course, you may find yourself spending more time in class preparation. Teaching is a time-hog in the sense that it takes a great deal of preparation to teach well and graduate students often find themselves spending an inordinate amount of time on their teaching. While learning how to teach well is an important skill, especially if you want to work in academia after graduate school, it can delay your graduation because time spent teaching is lost research time. As a graduate student, research is your mission. Your graduation will depend on developing a dissertation that's unique and well-researched. That's no small task and will require extensive amounts of time.

Research Assistantship

Research assistants get excellent research training because they're paid to assist professors in conducting their research. Usually research assistants are paid from a professor's research grants and work closely with him or her for about 20 hours per week. As a research assistant you may be asked to:

- travel off-campus to collect data for the professor's research
- copy articles, surveys, and other materials
- conduct literature searches
- write literature reviews and drafts of presentations
- prepare reference lists
- conduct statistical analyses

Essentially, you may become involved in any or all parts of a professor's research, including publications, which can be a fantastic benefit to becoming a research assistant. Generally if you have a choice between a teaching and research assistantship, it's better to go for the research assistantship, which pays you to conduct research and advance your career. There's plenty of time for teaching later, but whether you complete graduate school, and whether you're able to secure an academic position after graduate school is dependent on your research experience and particularly your publication record. A research assistantship is a paid opportunity to develop your publication record, so look at it as more than a job—it's a professional opportunity.

Exhibit 4 offers more tips from graduate students on how to obtain funding for graduate study. We've discussed just the tip of the iceberg when it comes to sources of financial aid. There are a variety of scholarships and fellowships that are available through institutional, state, and private funding sources. A variety of books list scholarship and fellowship opportunities and there are a number of excellent websites that cover this material as well (check out the resources in the appendix at the end of this book). Be a financial aid sleuth because there's "gold" out there—you just need to be thorough and search out all the sources.

Exhibit 3. Sample Curriculum Vitae

ALFRED E. NEWPORT
212 West 52nd Street
New York, NY 11012
(212) 254-9899
Newman@newman.com

Education

1993–1994	Master of Arts, Freak University
1988–1993	Bachelor of Arts, College of Rhode Island
Major: Psychology

Honors/Fellowships

1994–1995	Presidential Scholarship, Freak University
1993–present	Member of Psi Chi, National Honors Society for Psychology
1992	Who's Who Among Students in American Universities and Colleges

Professional Affiliations

American Psychological Association

Experience

1995–1996	Research Assistant, New York City Department for the Unstable
Conducted content analysis of qualitative data in a study on senior center satisfaction of older adults. Other responsibilities include interviewing older adults, data auditing, and literature review.
1994–1995	Lab Assistant, Freak University
Instructed students in Introduction to Psychology Lab and Perception Lab. Responsibilities included creating and/or supervising educational lab projects, grading homework assignments, exams, and papers.

1993–1994	Tutor in Psychology, Freak University Higher Education Opportunity Program
	Tutored undergraduate psychology students in Introduction to Psychology, Research Methods, and Statistics
1992–1993	Tutor in Psychology, College of Rhode Island
	Tutored undergraduate psychology students in Research Methods and Statistics
1990–1992	Residential Worker, Rhode Island Association for the Unstable
	Direct care and supervision of residents in a group home. Acted as a resident advocate.

Conference Presentations

Newman, A. E., & Higfish, C. B. Effects of social support from family and friends on adaptation to insanity. Paper to be presented at the annual meeting of the State Society on Insanity of New York, Albany, NY, October, 1997.

Newman, A. E., & Higfish, C. B. Effects of coping on individuals with insanity and instability. Paper presented at the annual meeting of the Eastern Psychological Association, Washington, DC, April, 1997.

Sugar, E. T., Higfish, C. B., & Newman, A. E. Expected utility predictors of sexual activity and instability. Paper presented at the Sixth International Conference on Insanity Education, Washington DC, August, 1992.

Exhibit 4. Tips from Graduate Students

- Be aggressive in seeking funding. Even if you have to take out loans, remember that it's worth it to pursue the career you desire. The department office and financial aid office at your graduate school can provide names and websites that have helped other students.
- Definitely ask questions about what kind of financial aid the program offers. Find out about summer funding. Are you expected to

take summer classes? Will you have an assistantship? Some programs expect you to take out loans to cover living expenses. If there aren't funding opportunities, find out what other students do.

- Look into small grants. Don't assume that you won't be able to get any funding. There is a lot of money out there waiting to be taken. Try for everything because every little bit helps. Also, be prepared to live like a student. You'll work a lot of hours and not make much money. Learn to live on a budget.
- Explore every option possible. Do research and you'll find that there are a lot of scholarships, grants, and other funding opportunities available from outside sources and within universities from avenues other than your department. If you have to take out loans, go for those that are specifically for education because they usually have low interest rates. As soon as you know that you want to go to graduate school, start saving!
- Before you accept funding, find out what you must do to obtain it. Assistantships require you to be a research or teaching assistant, but that is experience that most graduate students want anyway. Some fellowships are tied to specific projects and specific fields, which may require your thesis or dissertation to be tied to a specific topic.
- Remember that loans can be paid off and education is an investment. Get your education now, while you have the opportunity, and put off buying that new CD, video game, or other toy until you can do so without sacrificing your education.
- Ask! Originally I wasn't funded and was prepared to go into a truckload of debt. I asked the director of my program and he told me that there was full funding for one student floating around because an accepted applicant deferred for one year thus leaving her funding available. You can also see if the graduate school itself has funding opportunities. I know of people who obtained full funding for working for the library because that's what the university needed that year. Talk to other students too and see what options there are. Find out how successful graduate students manage financially and mimic them.

Chapter 5

THE GRADUATE RECORD EXAM

Most graduate school applicants dread the Graduate Record Exam (GRE). What is the GRE and why does it cause so much anxiety in applicants? In this chapter, we'll discuss the Graduate Record Exam, what it is, how to prepare, and how to keep your anxiety at bay and perform your best.

THE GRE GENERAL TEST

The GRE measures a variety of skills that are thought to predict success in graduate school. Actually, there are several GRE tests. Usually when an applicant, professor, or admissions director mentions the GRE, he or she is referring to the GRE General Test. Many, but not all, psychology graduate programs also require applicants to take the GRE Subject Test in Psychology, an achievement test that measures your knowledge of psychological facts and concepts. We'll talk more about the GRE Psychology Test later in this chapter, but first, let's focus on the GRE General Test, which is the more critical and commonly required exam.

The GRE General Test is an aptitude test because it is meant to assess your potential to succeed in graduate school by measuring the skills that you've acquired over the high school and college years. While the GRE is only one of several criteria that graduate schools use to evaluate your application, it is one of the most important. This is particularly true if your college grade point average (GPA) is not as high as you'd like. Exceptional GRE scores can open up new opportunities for graduate school. Plus GRE scores often are used in assigning funding to new students (and we've seen how expensive graduate school can be!).

The GRE General Test contains sections that measure verbal, quantitative, and analytical skills. The verbal section tests your ability to understand and analyze written material and synthesize information obtained from it through the use of analogies, antonyms, sentence completions, and reading comprehension questions. The quantitative section evaluates basic mathematical skills and your ability to understand and apply quantitative skills to solve problems. Types of questions include quantitative comparisons, problem solving, and data interpretation. The analytical writing section assesses your ability to articulate complex ideas clearly and effectively, examine claims and accompanying evidence, support ideas with relevant reasons and examples, sustain a well-focused, coherent discussion, and control the elements of standard written English. It consists of two written essays: a 45-minute "Present Your Perspective on an Issue" task and a 30-minute "Analyze an Argument" task.

The verbal and quantitative subtests yield scores ranging from 200 to 800. Most graduate schools consider the verbal and quantitative sections to be particularly important in making decisions about applicants. The analytical writing subtest yields a score ranging from 0 to 6. The analytical writing section is new to the GRE (adopted in 2002) and many admissions committees are unfamiliar with it, so it isn't easy to predict how committees will evaluate analytical writing scores; however, graduate study in psychology requires analytical thinking, therefore it's in your best interest to prepare for this section and perform as well as possible.

GRE General Test Facts

The GRE General Test is administered only by computer year-round (a pencil and paper version is offered in several countries outside of the United States where technological security is a risk to the integrity of the test). Register for the GRE General Test by phone (1-800-GRE-CALL, or 1-800-473-2255) or by mail using the address and registration form found in the GRE Information and Registration Bulletin (at http://gre.org). Remember that appointments are assigned on a first-come first-served basis, so register early.

When you register for the GRE, you'll select among several test administration centers at colleges, universities, and testing centers. For a complete list of testing centers, consult the GRE website at http://etsis4.ets.org/tcenter/. In 2003, registration for the General Test cost $115 within the United States, U.S. Territories, and Puerto Rico, and $140 in all other locations.

Arrive at the test center at least 30 minutes early to complete any paperwork. If you arrive late, you may not be admitted and will not be refunded. Remember to bring at least two forms of identification (with at least one containing a photo and signature). For more information about identification requirements and policies, consult the GRE Information and Registration Bulletin. The GRE General Test will take two and one-quarter hours to complete, but allow an extra hour and one-half for reading instructions and taking tutorials.

When Should You Take the GRE General Test?

Plan to take the GRE well in advance of application due dates. Try to take it the spring or summer before you apply to grad school (i.e., the end of your junior year). You can always retake the GRE, but remember that you're allowed to take it only once per calendar month. Because all prior scores are sent to the institutions to which you're applying, never take the GRE as practice.

Verbal Section of the GRE

You will be administered two or three verbal sections when you take the GRE General (if you're administered three, then one is a test section designed to evaluate new questions and will not count towards your score; however there is no way to determine which, if any, of the verbal sections are test versions). The verbal section consists of 30 multiple choice questions that are answered within 30 minutes. That's not a lot of time, so it's important to be familiar with the test so that you can work quickly and efficiently. In other words, practice beforehand using the *POWERPREP* software provided by Gre.org as well as the books and websites recommended at the end of this chapter.

Within the verbal section, you will be asked to read passages and analyze information obtained from your reading, analyze sentences and the relationships among component parts of sentences, as well as recognize relationships between words and concepts within written material. The topics that comprise the reading comprehension sections are meant to be answered without any particular knowledge or expertise, other than the general knowledge and skills that an average graduate is presumed to have. Excelling on the verbal section of the GRE requires an advanced vocabulary.

There are four types of questions: analogies, antonyms, reading comprehension, and sentence completion. Let's take a closer look at each.

- Analogies examine your ability to understand the relationship that exists between the words in a word pair and recognize a parallel relationship among other word pairs. This requires determining how two words are related and then determining what word pair provided displays a similar relationship.
- Antonyms test your knowledge of vocabulary and your ability to identify the opposite of a given concept.
- Comprehension measures your ability to read analytically. You're asked to explore a written passage from several perspectives, recognize elements that are explicitly stated and inferred, and understand the assumptions underlying the passage as well as the implications of those assumptions. Reading comprehension questions assess six types of information: identify the main idea, identify explicitly stated information, identify implied ideas, apply the author's ideas to other situations, identify the author's logic or persuasive techniques, and identify the attitudinal tone of the passage.
- Sentence completion questions measure your ability to use syntax and grammar cues to understand the meaning of a sentence. This task requires that you analyze the parts of the incomplete sentence and determine which word or set of words can be substituted for the blank space in the sentence.

Quantitative Section of the GRE

The GRE General Test contains two quantitative sections (three if a new set of quantitative questions are being tested). The quantitative section consists of 28 multiple choice questions that are completed within 45 minutes. The quantitative section measures "basic mathematical skills, and understanding of mathematical concepts, as well as the ability to reason quantitatively and to solve problems in a quantitative setting" (GRE Bulletin, p. 5). Essentially, the quantitative section does not require mathematic skills beyond the high school level (e.g., arithmetic, algebra, geometry, and data analysis); but calculators are not permitted, so you must be prepared to complete problems only with the help of a pencil and scratch paper. The quantitative section is composed of three types of questions, problem solving, quantitative comparison, and data analysis. Let's take a look at each type of question:

- Problem solving questions are word problems that assess your understanding of, and ability to apply, arithmetic, algebra, and geometry.
- Quantitative comparison questions ask you to compare two quantities, one in column a and one in column b. Your task is to determine if they are equal, if one is larger than the other, or if not enough information is presented to make the determination.
- Data analysis questions require use of basic descriptive statistics, the ability to interpret data in graphs and tables, and elementary probability. Questions emphasize the "ability to synthesize information, select appropriate data for answering a question, and to determine whether or not the data provided are sufficient to answer a given question" (GRE Bulletin, p. 8).

Analytical Writing Section of the GRE

The analytical writing section examines your ability to communicate complex ideas clearly and effectively, support your ideas, examine claims and supporting evidence, sustain a focused and coherent discussion, and effectively use the elements of standard written English. There are two subsections:

- Present Your Perspective on an Issue. In this 45-minute task, you are presented with an issue of general interest and asked to address it from any perspective, providing reasons and examples to support your views. Your job is to construct an argument and support it with reasons and examples.

- Analyze an Argument. This 30-minute task presents you with an argument. Your task is to critique the argument, assess its claims, and conclude whether it is reasoned.

Like the other sections of the GRE General, the essay tasks are delivered on the computer. The GRE software contains a simple word processor that includes basic functions like cut and paste, insert text, delete, and undo, but does not include spelling or grammar checkers. Practice using the word processor on *POWERPREP*, the practice software sent to you when you register for the GRE (and downloadable from the GRE website at http://gre.org).

Scoring of the GRE

Your score on the GRE depends on how well you performed on the questions given and on the total number of questions answered in the time allotted. Because the GRE is a computer adaptive test (CAT), later questions are selected based on your performance on earlier questions as well as the overall test design (e.g., the required variety of question types and the appropriate coverage of content). The verbal and quantitative sections are reported on a 200 to 800 score scale, in ten-point increments. If you take the GRE by computer, you will receive your unofficial verbal and quantitative scores immediately after completing the test. You won't receive your analytical writing scores immediately because the analytical writing task must be scored by hand. Official scores will be sent to you and the institutions you designate within ten to 15 days of test administration. Verbal, quantitative, and analytical writing scores on the computer-based General Test will be sent to you and the institutions you designate within ten to 15 days of your test administration.

The analytical writing section is scored the same whether your responses are typed into the computer or handwritten. Two trained readers assess each essay on a 6-point scale. They use holistic scoring, which means that they assign scores on the basis of the overall quality of your essay in response to the assignment. If the two scores differ by more than one point, then a third reader is called in. Final scores on the two essays are averaged and rounded up to the nearest half-point to provide a single score for the section. The emphasis is on examining your critical thinking and analytical writing skills rather than grammar.

Preparing for the GRE General Test

The best advice that I can give on preparing to take the GRE General Test is to begin early to ensure that you earn the highest score possible. This is not the time to cram!

- Buy a GRE review book. See the suggestions in the appendix at the end of this book.
- Download sample GRE tests. The appendix provides links to several websites that offer free sample tests.
- Download *GRE POWERPREP Software–Test Preparation for the GRE General Test,* free software provided by the makers of the GRE. According to the online description, *POWERPREP* "includes test tutorials, practice questions with explanations, and two actual computer-adaptive tests for the verbal and quantitative sections. The software also includes sample topics and essays for the analytical writing section, and advice on how to write effective essays for the Issue and Argument tasks. *POWERPREP* lets you practice writing essays under simulated GRE testing conditions with the same GRE word processing and testing tools that appear on the test" (at http://www.gre.org/faqnew.html)
- Try a practice test under conditions similar to the actual GRE. Based on your practice score, devise a study plan to help you brush up on vocabulary, reading comprehension, analogies, algebra, and geometry.
- Know the test. Your GRE preparation should emphasize getting to know the test and the types of questions that will appear. Be familiar with the time limit for each section and how many questions each section includes.
- Know the directions for each question beforehand to save time, but remember that the directions for the GRE Test might be slightly different from the ones in your study material. So be sure to always read the instructions–quickly.

Before the Test

- If you're taking the GRE at a test center other than at your college or university, do a test drive the week before to learn where the center is and how long it takes to arrive because it's important that you get to the test center 30 minutes beforehand.

- Get enough sleep the night before. Sure, it's hard to relax when you have a big exam, but it's essential that you unwind. Don't study the night before. Instead, have a quiet night at home and do something that you find relaxing and enjoyable.
- Eat breakfast. Make sure that you're not hungry during the test, which can affect your performance.
- Wear comfortable clothes and bring a sweater in case the test center is cold.

On Test Day

- Your practice should make you familiar with the test and the amount of time you need to tackle each type of question. Don't get stuck on one particular question for too long because you'll lose time and may miss easier questions later on.
- Don't rush. The GRE isn't a race, so use your time judiciously, devoting just enough time to each question to get it done and maximize your score in the limited time allotted.
- Remember that the questions at the beginning of the exam are more important than those toward the end. Because the GRE is computer adaptive, the difficulty level of the questions you receive later are determined by those you've correctly answered before.
- If you don't know the answer to a question, use the method of elimination and eliminate alternatives that cannot be the answer to narrow down your guesses to two or three alternatives and improve the odds of choosing correctly.
- Don't leave questions unanswered because there is no penalty for wrong answers.
- Be very sure of your answer before proceeding. With the Computer-Adaptive Test (CAT) for GRE, you cannot return to a question once you have attempted it. You cannot leave the difficult questions for later nor can you check your answers towards the end even if you have extra time. So pace yourself properly and be very certain of your answers.

Should You Ever Retake the GRE?

According to the American Psychological Association (1997) the average minimum GRE scores required for serious consideration by doctoral programs is about 550 per section and 1200 total (combined verbal and quantitative scores). Now remember that there's much more to your application than your GRE scores and even if your scores are lower than the average there is still the possibility that you may be considered for doctoral programs if you have significant other strengths and experiences (like substantial research experience, for example).

Generally you should only retake the GRE if you can score demonstrably higher next time. Most people get roughly similar scores each time they take the GRE (it has high test-retest reliability), so only retake the GRE if your initial score was negatively influenced by something like illness, extreme anxiety, or inadequate preparation and if you can improve your score by at least 30 points per section. Remember that all scores are reported, not just your best scores, so never take the GRE as practice. If you believe that you didn't perform well, you can have your scores cancelled if you indicate so at the end of your exam and BEFORE you receive your unofficial scores.

GRE SUBJECT TEST IN PSYCHOLOGY

The GRE Psychology Test assesses your knowledge of psychological content emphasized by undergraduate programs as preparation for graduate education. Not all graduate programs require that you take the GRE Psychology Test, so before registering for it make sure that you've checked with the programs to which you're applying.

GRE Psychology Test Facts

The GRE Psychology Test is administered by pencil and paper three times a year: November, December, and April. Register for the GRE Psychology Test by phone (1-800-GRE-CALL, or 1-800-473-2255) or by mail using the address and registration form found in the GRE Information and Registration Bulletin (at http://gre.org). Remember that seats are assigned on a first-come first-served basis, so register early.

When you register for the GRE, you'll select among several test administration centers at colleges, universities, and testing centers. For a complete list of testing centers, consult the GRE website. In 2003, registration for the GRE Psychology Test cost $130 within the United States, U.S. Territories, and Puerto Rico, and $150 in all other locations. The instructions regarding arriving early and bringing proper identification provided earlier for the GRE General Test also apply to the GRE Psychology Test. The test takes up to three and one-half hours to complete.

Content of the GRE Psychology Test

The GRE Psychology Test consists of about 215 multiple choice questions. The questions are drawn from commonly offered courses at the undergraduate level and are designed to measure what an undergraduate Psychology major who plans to attend graduate school should know about the field of Psychology. Questions cover the following categories of content (Matlin & Kalat, 2001):

- Experimental psychology topics (about 40 percent of the test), such as learning, language, memory, thinking, sensation and perception, physiological psychology, ethology, and comparative psychology.
- Clinical and social topics (about 43 percent of the test), including clinical and abnormal, developmental, personality, and social psychology.
- General psychology topics (about 17 percent of the test), such as the history of psychology, measurement, research designs, and statistics.

Since the GRE Psychology Test is designed to sample a broad overview of topics in psychology, the best way to prepare is by studying an upper-level Introductory Psychology textbook, such as *Psychology*, by Fridlund, Reisburg, and Gleitman, or *Psychology: In Search of the Human Mind*, by Robert J. Sternberg. Take the GRE Psychology Test in October of your senior year (to benefit from all of the psychology courses that you've taken beforehand).

CONQUERING TEST ANXIETY

Lots of students get nervous when they take important tests like the GRE. While a little bit of nervousness can help you to focus, pay attention, and perform well, a lot of anxiety can harm your performance. Symptoms of severe test anxiety include:

- Headache
- Nausea or diarrhea
- Faintness
- Out of breath or feeling like your heart is beating too fast
- Blanking out
- Feeling like you're going to cry
- Feelings of fear or anger
- Muscle tension
- Feeling overwhelmed

How can you control test anxiety?

- Be well prepared. Begin studying for the GRE months beforehand so that you're familiar with the structure of the test and its content. Preparation is the antidote to test anxiety.
- Get enough sleep the night before.
- Take slow deep breaths when you first sit down to calm yourself before the exam.
- Use the tutorial to calm yourself. Before the GRE begins, you have the option to take a GRE tutorial designed to familiarize you with the software and format of the test. Take advantage of the tutorial and use it to calm yourself and get used to your surroundings.
- Focus on the exam. If your mind wanders, bring it back immediately. If needed, you might mark a piece of scrap paper each time your mind wanders as a signal to remember to focus on the exam.
- If you feel yourself getting tense, take deep breaths, roll your head and shoulders to combat muscle tension and close your eyes. Do this between each section of the GRE (the clock stops between sections).
- Use positive self-talk. Tell yourself, "I know I can do this. I'll be ok."

Sure the GRE is stressful, but you can take control of your experience if you understand the test and begin preparing early. Consult the books and resources in the appendix of this book, as well as the advice from graduate students in Exhibit 5 for more specific tips that will help you to perform your best on the Graduate Record Exam.

Exhibit 5. Tips from Graduate Students

- I prepared through independent studying and a prep class. The only thing I would do differently is to take advantage of all opportunities and spend more time studying on my own.
- I took a course. It was sort of helpful. If you've ever taken a prep course for the SAT, it's probably not worth the money to take one for the GRE as the strategies are similar. If you are disciplined and can make yourself sit down and go over the material on your own, just set up a schedule, buy a good review book, and go for it. If you need more structure, a course will force you to study.
- I spent three months studying with a review book. I wish I spent more time studying because I did ok–not super. I would have prepared at least six months ahead of time.
- Two to three hours per day for three months was the time that I put into studying. I took practice tests and honed in on my weak areas.
- If I could do it again, I'd do more practice tests on the computer. Taking it on the computer is really different from the written practice tests.
- For the quantitative section, I studied geometry and algebra. The material is easy, but most of us haven't been exposed to it in years. Review! For the verbal section, I learned the words suggested in popular review books. Most of them actually appeared on the test. Also take practice tests on the web.
- If I could do it again, I'd relax more. I got into a program I love and could have done it without freaking out so much over the GRE. You can too.

Chapter 6

PERSONAL STATEMENTS AND ADMISSIONS ESSAYS

No aspect of the graduate admissions process generates more confusion on the part of applicants than the admissions essay, also known as the personal statement. The admissions essay is your opportunity to talk directly with the admissions committee, to call attention to important parts of your application that might otherwise be overlooked, and to explain any discrepancies or potentially negative aspects of your application. It's your chance to help the admissions committee see you as a person instead of a grade point average and a clump of standardized test scores. On paper, many applicants look identical: good grades and high GRE scores. Admissions committees need the additional information provided in admissions essays to narrow the pool of applicants. Your essays will tell the committee about your ability to write, to stick to the task at hand, and to persuade readers. Your essay will also inform the admissions committee about your interests, career aspirations, and values. This is the place where you can make yourself stand out from the crowd.

Most students find writing the personal statement challenging because it's an ambiguous task. Some students freeze when they begin to write the essay—or just put it off and write it at the last minute. Don't fall into these traps. Instead, carefully plan your essay and devote the necessary time to writing an essay that you can be proud of and that will win you admission to the school of your choice. The admissions essay cannot be written in a day or two, it will require weeks, if not months, of preparation. In this chapter you'll learn how to approach the admissions essay or personal statement, but first, let's talk about the kinds of essays that are required by admissions committees.

ESSAY TOPICS: WHAT CAN YOU EXPECT TO WRITE ABOUT?

Some graduate school applications don't specify the topic of the essay; they simply request an autobiographical statement. Others provide more firm guidelines on what topics applicants are to compose their personal statements. Keith-Spiegel and Wiederman (2000) examined a wide range of graduate school applications and noticed a remarkable similarity among essay topics, as categorized below:

- *Career Plans.* What are your long-term career goals? Where do you see yourself, career-wise, ten years from now?
- *Academic Interests.* What would you like to study? Describe your academic interests. Which professors in the department would you like to work with?
- *Research Experiences.* Discuss your research experiences. What areas would you like to research?
- *Academic Objectives.* Why do you plan to attend graduate school? Explain how graduate school will contribute to your career goals. What do you plan to do with your degree?
- *Clinical and Field Experience.* Discuss your clinical and other applied experiences. How have these experiences shaped your career goals?
- *Academic Achievements.* Discuss your academic background and achievements.
- *Personal Experience.* Write an autobiographical essay. Is there anything in your background that you think would be relevant to your application for admission to graduate school? Describe your life up to now: family, friends, home, school, work, and particularly those experiences most relevant to your interests in psychology. What is your approach to life?

You'll probably find that most of your applications require similar kinds of essays, but this doesn't mean that you should write a generic essay for all of the programs to which you're applying. With today's word processing software, tailoring your admissions essays to specific graduate programs is easy. By tailoring your essay to the particular program, you can show how your interests and abilities match the program and faculty.

ON THE AUTOBIOGRAPHICAL STATEMENT

Perhaps the most difficult admissions essay to write is one in which no topic is given: the autobiographical statement. Some graduate school applications will request that you "tell us something about yourself" or simply "submit a personal statement." Where do you start with such an amorphous assignment? What do you reveal about yourself? It's easy to get overwhelmed when you're provided with minimal instructions, so instead provide your own direction. An effective autobiographical statement doesn't start by explaining your birth or early childhood, instead it describes significant experiences that have made you who you are today, shaped your goals, and defined your interests in psychology. What is the admissions committee looking for when it requests such an ambiguous statement? Essentially, an autobiographical essay should include an explanation of your interests in psychology and how they developed, a discussion of your career goals within the field of psychology, and how your interests match the training provided by the program to which you're applying (Hayes & Hayes, 1989).

Your personal statement should be an organized and well-written essay in which you describe how you decided to enter psychology, and what academic, research, applied, and life experiences you've had that confirm your interests and aptitude for a career in psychology. Many students explain that they wish to enter graduate study in psychology in order to help people. Wanting to help people isn't a good enough reason to undertake graduate study—it's too vague. Be specific. How do you want to help people? Why? What is the problem that you'd like to address? Use this as an opportunity to link your emotional motivation with your intellectual and academic interests. The essay should illustrate that you've carefully considered your career choice and that it's a logical extension of your experiences and interests to date. Convey your determination to pursue your career goals and that the program to which you are applying will maximize your ability to pursue your goals.

Discuss college and work experiences that are relevant to your intended career. Perhaps you volunteered in a nursing home, or got a part-time job at a psychiatric hospital. Only go into detail about these experiences if they are specifically relevant to your intended career and you can make the connection explicit. Be sure to discuss your research experience, the kinds of responsibilities you had, and what you learned. Describe your research interests—which is an understandably difficult task for many students. Remember that you're not promising or committing yourself to do the research you describe, but are showing the committee that you know what research is and that you have interests in research. Also be sure to read about the department and faculty so that you can explain how your interests match those of the faculty. If you mention that your interests match those of a particular faculty member, be sure to read his or her work and discuss how your interests coincide with the faculty member so that it is clear that you have read his or her research and are not just name-dropping.

Describe specific educational and occupational experiences that are the basis for your interest in psychology and try your best to avoid discussing personal (i.e., nonacademic or nonprofessional) experiences. This is not the time to talk about your own or a family member's problems. The admissions committee will use your essay to determine whether you're suitable for graduate study. Don't self-disclose personal information that might be construed negatively. This is not the time to explain that your interest in psychology stems from your dysfunctional family or to learn more about your own history of pathology and/or mental illness (Kuther & Morgan, 2004).

If extenuating circumstances have influenced your performance in college or on standardized tests, consider discussing them in your personal statement, but be careful to consider how your excuses will be perceived. For example, explaining poor grades for one semester by briefly mentioning a death in the family or serious illness is appropriate; however, an attempt to explain four years of poor grades is not likely to be successful. If you perform poorly on tests and wish to explain that to the committee, be sure to have a reason for your poor performance in hand (e.g., dyslexia, another learning disability, or not a native speaker of English). Simply explaining that you don't test well will not help your application as most graduate programs entail many tests. Keep all excuses and explanations to a minimum—a sentence or two. Avoid drama and keep it simple. Remember that this is your chance to present your strengths and really shine, so take advantage of the opportunity to discuss your accomplishments, describe valuable experiences, and emphasize the positive.

ADMISSIONS ESSAY AS PROCESS

Writing your admissions essay is a process, not a discrete event. The first step involves preparation, gathering the information needed to compose a personal essay that sets you apart from the rest.

Assess Yourself

Conduct a thorough self-assessment to pull together all of the information, examples, and details that you'll need to compose your essay. Begin your personal assessment months before your essay is due because self-exploration is a process that you can't rush. Sit down with a pad, or at the keyboard, and begin writing. Don't censor yourself in any way. Just write what feels natural. Who are you? What drives you? What are your hopes, dreams, and aspirations? What do you hope to gain from graduate study? In what ways are you special? Brainstorm. Not all of this information will make it into your admissions essay. Instead, your goal is to identify possibilities—what kinds of information might you include in your essay? Identify as much of your personal history as possible so that you can carefully sift through and sort out events and personal items that will strengthen your essay. As you brainstorm, consider:

- your hobbies
- major class projects that you've completed
- jobs you've held
- responsibilities you manage
- personal accomplishments (e.g., completing a marathon)
- academic accomplishments
- major life events that have changed you
- challenges and hurdles you've overcome
- life events that motivate your education
- people who have influenced you or motivated you
- traits, work habits, and attitudes that will insure your success your goals

In addition to these prompts, answer the questions in Exhibit 6 to expand your list of potential essay topics.

Once your brainstorming has generated a large list, carefully examine the information that you've listed. Remember that the information that you choose to present can portray you in a positive light–as a curious and eager student, or in a negative light–as a tired and discouraged student. Think about the image that you want to portray and revise your list of experiences, traits, and accomplishments accordingly. Use the revised list as a basis for all of your admissions essays. What items on your list can be used to illustrate that you're an excellent candidate for graduate study?

Review Your List of Programs

Carefully review the programs that interest you so that you can tailor your essays to each program. Read the brochure, check the website, and learn about the faculty members' research interests to help you determine what the admissions committee is looking for from potential students. Your research should provide enough of a knowledge base about the department and program to tailor your essay to it. Take careful notes on each program, especially how your personal interests, qualities, and accomplishments coincide with program goals and curricula. If you're truly interested in the graduate programs to which you're applying (and with a $50 application fee for most schools, you should be interested!), take the time to tailor your essay to each program because one size does not fit all. Tailoring your essay to the specific program to which you're applying shows that you're interested and that you've taken the time to learn about the program and allows you to showcase how well you match the program.

Getting Started: Dealing with Writer's Block

Once you've listed your personal attributes and experiences and have researched programs, it's time to start writing. Having a hard time starting your personal statement? Don't worry. Nearly everyone faces writer's block when it comes time to write the personal statement for graduate school admissions. Here's what you can do to get started writing your personal statement.

Too many applicants get tongue-tied at the first sentence of their personal statements. Just how do you start? Worry about crafting a magnificent opening sentence to your essay later. You don't have to start writing at the beginning of your essay and work your way through to the end. Begin anywhere it feels right. In fact, I tell my own students to begin with a bullet-point list of the points to be made and then construct the personal statement around those points.

Since the personal statement is your opportunity to stand out, you might begin by talking about the one thing that makes you different from all of the other applicants. Or you might begin by talking about an experience that was important to you. How did you become interested in your discipline? How did you know that you wanted to go to graduate school? Write about some of your activities: why did you start them and what motivates you about them?

Don't worry about what you're writing and don't edit as you go. Instead, just write–anything. Don't feel wedded to what you write, but consider writing as a process in which you can discover what you'd like to include in your essay. Remember that you're writing the first of many drafts. You'll improve and strengthen your essay with each draft, but the hardest one to write is the first draft. Don't censor or edit your writing as you compose your first draft–just get all of your ideas on paper. Each time you revise your essay, add supporting details and evaluate the logic and flow of your writing but don't begin the revision process until you've completed a first draft.

Remember to Respond to the Questions Posed

It's easy to digress when writing, so each time you edit your essay take a step back and consider whether you're responding to the questions posed. Think about the question, the central theme asked, and how it corresponds to your master list of experiences/personal qualities. Some applications offer a string of questions. Pay attention to your responses and try to avoid being redundant. As you write your essay, remember that you're telling a story. You should cite past experiences that made you interested in psychology, how you've obtained additional experience to bolster your application, and why you seek to attend graduate school.

Revising and Polishing Your Essay

Once you have a full draft of your essay, let it sit for a few hours or a day, and then begin revising it. Outline what you've written. Are your points in a logical order? Do all of your points make sense and support your argument? Determine the major theme of your essay. Add details and examples (e.g., provide examples of specific responsibilities you've held or ways that you've helped your advisor advance his or her research). Ask yourself:

- Does my essay include information already discussed in another section of the application?
- Does my essay accurately describe my best attributes without sounding superficial?
- Does my essay communicate a clear sense of purpose?
- Are the words I use descriptive and engaging?
- Are the personal details I discuss relevant to my success as a potential graduate student?
- Are there any understatements that need clarification?
- Do I appear to have long-range plans? Does graduate school seem like the key to obtaining my long-term goals? Have I presented a logical rationale for my interest in graduate study?

Get feedback on your writing from as many people as you can. Ask professors to provide comments. They can guide you on what to focus on, what to eliminate, and so on. Also consider getting feedback before your essay is finished so that you can correct and revise it before you've spent too much time on it. Your reader might see potential in an idea that you were about to trash and might help you to stay on track. When you think you're done, give yourself time away from your essay and you'll come back to it with a fresh eye, with the ability to objectively evaluate your essay. Read your essay aloud to check for omissions and errors and get a friend to check for grammar and spelling errors.

When your essay is complete, you should be inspired and proud. Reread your personal statement to be sure that it discusses your strengths. It's sometimes hard for us to talk about ourselves as we're often taught that modesty is a virtue–but it isn't when you're applying to graduate school. It's ok to feel like you're being boastful or even cheesy, as long as what you've written is true. Your goal in writing your personal statement should be to excite and inspire your reader–and get a ticket to graduate school.

MORE ADMISSIONS ESSAY TIPS

- Carefully read the instructions for each application. Programs pose different questions for applicants. Some applications will request you to address several topics and others might simply ask for a general statement of purpose.
- Be forthcoming about your weaknesses. If your early academic record is weak, explain why and how you've overcome your weaknesses.
- Don't go over the specified word limit. If no length guidelines are offered, stick to 500 to 1,000 words.
- Give yourself lots of time to write and revise your essay.
- Be sure to highlight how well you match the program.
- Showcase your strengths.
- Be honest and don't exaggerate.
- Avoid jargon.
- Be concise.
- Read your essay out loud to catch errors and awkwardness.
- Get lots of help.
- Don't discuss personal problems.
- Keep it positive.
- Don't make grammar or spelling errors.
- Avoid attempts at humor. You'll come across as sophomoric and not serious about your career.
- Don't discuss your achievements or accomplishments prior to college.
- Don't discuss controversial topics as you don't know who will be reading your essay or how you might offend them. Avoid discussing politics, religion, or anything that might be considered bizarre (e.g., your own or a family member's mental health problems).
- Don't mention a desire to work with a particular faculty member unless you have read his or her papers and are prepared to refer to the faculty member in a way that demonstrates your understanding of his or her work. The reader must be able to tell that you've actually read the papers and are knowledgeable about the faculty member's work or the tactic of aligning yourself with a particular faculty member will backfire.

- Don't feel bad if you don't have a lot of experience in psychology to write about. Explain your relevant experiences and understand that most students don't have a great deal of psychology-related experiences to talk about–so don't try to overinflate your own experiences.

Exhibit 6. Questions to Consider as You Prepare Your Essay

Write about the following questions to learn more about yourself and gather information to use in your admissions essays.

- What are your career goals? Where do you see yourself in ten years?
- Why did you choose psychology? What areas of psychology interest you and why?
- Which professors in the department would you like to work with and why? (Responding to this question requires some research on your part.)
- Describe your experience with research.
- Describe a research topic that you'd like to study. If you were to design a research study, what would it be on?
- What role does graduate study play in your career goals?
- Discuss your clinically related experiences. What applied experiences have you had and how have they influenced your decision to attend graduate school?
- Of what academic achievements are you most proud?
- What personal experiences have influenced your decision to attend graduate school in psychology?
- What experiences have made you who you are today?
- How did you choose to major in psychology? (Or, if you've majored in something other than psychology, why did you choose it and why are you seeking to attend graduate school in psychology or a related field?)
- Describe your work experiences. How do they fit with your decision to attend graduate school?
- What personal qualities do you have that will help you to excel in graduate school?

- What personal qualities do you have that might make graduate school a challenge?
- How are you special?
- Why should you be admitted to graduate school? What benefits do you offer faculty?
- Describe your hobbies and interests.
- Describe a personal accomplishment of which you're proud.
- What challenges have you overcome?
- Describe a person or people who have influenced you.

Exhibit 7. Tips from Graduate Students

- Personal statements work the best when students take the opportunity to address weaknesses and outline their strengths. Show your personality. Reviewers will appreciate your authenticity and get a better sense of who you are, beyond your grades and accomplishments. Now that I'm in graduate school I realize that faculty are interested in students who want to make investments in their future. They are looking for good matches to the faculty and staff.
- Be personal, but not casual. Tell them about yourself, what makes you unique, and why you have done the things that you have done.
- Be interesting but not controversial.
- Be honest in your personal statement. Don't exaggerate because it will make you look stupid later.
- Have someone else, preferably a faculty member, look over your statement for typos and things that don't make sense. My research advisor met with me several times to look over my personal statements and CV. They know what professors are looking for in these things and what is appropriate and inappropriate.
- Don't go on about personal matters. I've been told that writing things of a really personal nature is looked down upon.
- Get as many people as you can to read it and give feedback.
- When multiple faculty read it you get the benefit of multiple perspectives. While one faculty member may not remark on something, another may. With different ideas of how it should be, you can decide for yourself what feedback you want to respond to and what feedback you won't. Then resubmit to the same faculty and see what they say.

- Find a recent successful applicant and see what their personal statement was like. Look at the tone, style, and format they follow and see if it matches well with what you've done.
- This sounds cheesy, but it's helpful to do soul searching and really see if graduate school is what you want to do. Try to find life experiences that would tell someone why graduate school is the right thing for you. Tell your story in a lively and vivid way. Tell it in your own voice.
- The ideal personal statement incorporates personal details, graduate school ambitions, career strivings, and an interpretation of the model after which you want to fashion your career. For example, my personal statement discussed the biopsychosocial and scientist-practitioner models as I saw them relating to my career. It's a difficult balance to strike.

Chapter 7

LETTERS OF RECOMMENDATION

Many students are surprised to learn that nearly every graduate program requires applicants to submit several letters of recommendation with their applications. A letter of recommendation is a detailed letter, usually written by a faculty member, that discusses the personal qualities, accomplishments, and experiences that make you unique and perfect for the graduate programs to which you've applied. Don't underestimate the importance of recommendation letters. While your transcript, standardized test scores, and personal statement or admissions essay are vital components to your application, an excellent letter of recommendation can make up for weaknesses in any of these areas. A well written letter of recommendation provides admissions committees with information that isn't found elsewhere in the application—insight into you as a person.

WHAT DO ADMISSIONS COMMITTEES REQUEST?

Most graduate school applications include general instructions for referees (those who write your letters of recommendation) on what to include in the letter. Many programs also include forms for referees to complete. Usually referees are asked to comment on your academic ability and performance in class. If you're applying to a research-oriented program, referees will be instructed to comment on your skills and potential as a researcher. On the other hand, if you're applying to a program that emphasizes practice more than research (e.g., Psy.D. program), letters should discuss your counseling skills, potential, and experience. A good letter of recommendation demonstrates that the referee knows you well and can provide details and examples to illustrate your abilities and potential to succeed. Therefore, it's important that your referees know you well. Later on in this chapter we'll talk about how to establish relationships with professors, but first, let's take a look at the types of info that graduate admissions committees look for in letters of recommendation. Typically, professors are asked to evaluate applicants'

- oral communication skills
- written communication skills
- critical thinking ability
- interpersonal skills and ability to work with others
- leadership ability
- ability to work independently
- academic performance
- commitment to the field
- motivation and initiative
- intellectual ability
- integrity
- maturity
- research potential
- teaching potential
- counseling skills and potential

Essentially, your letters must go beyond academics because graduate admissions committees will have your transcript and GRE scores. Instead, letters of recommendation describe you as a person and provide insight on what it would be like to know and work with you.

WHO TO ASK

Most graduate programs require two or more letters of recommendation. Choosing your letter writers often is difficult. Consider faculty members, administrators, internship/cooperative education supervisors, and employers. The persons you ask to write your letters should

- know you well
- know you long enough to write with authority
- know your work

- describe your work positively
- have a high opinion of you
- know where you are applying
- know your educational and career goals
- be able to favorably compare you with your peers
- be well known
- be able to write a good letter

Keep in mind that no one person will satisfy all of these criteria. Aim for a set of letters that cover the range of your skills. Ideally, letters should cover your academic and scholastic skills, research abilities and experiences, and applied experiences (e.g., cooperative education, internships, related work experience). Admissions committees are interested in letters from faculty who can describe your interest and ability with regard to research, how well you handle academic requirements, and your ability to work with others.

The most helpful letters of recommendation are from professors who know you well and have had contact with you in and outside of the classroom—especially in research. Sometimes students approach faculty from whom they've earned excellent grades but have had minimal contact outside of class. Such letters aren't very helpful because your academic information is available on your transcript, so the letter will add nothing new to your application. In fact, the letter can actually damage your application because it suggests that you've had little contact with your professors. In other words, the purpose of recommendation letters is not to attest to your excellent academic performance, which admissions committees can review from your transcript; instead, recommendation letters go beyond academic performance to describe your ability to perform well in graduate school and as a scholar. The best letters are from professors who have been involved with you professionally (who have supervised your research, asked you to help with his or her research, coauthored a paper with you, etc.).

Also note that the referee's credibility can influence how his or her letter is perceived. Letters from referees who have known you for several years hold more weight than those from referees who have known you only for a period of months. The referee's experience also influences his or her credibility. Most students aren't familiar with academic ranks, the various titles and positions that faculty may hold. *Adjunct professors* are part-time professors who teach only a course or two per semester They generally do not engage students in their research and have a very limited involvement in the department and university. *Assistant professors* are junior full-time faculty members. After several years, assistant professors who have demonstrated their competence in teaching and research are promoted to the rank of *associate professor.* *Full professors* are the most senior of faculty members who have a great deal of experience in academia. Generally, more senior faculty members are viewed as more credible by admissions committees—and they usually also have more experience writing letters of recommendation. Referee credibility and academic rank is secondary to the content of the recommendation letter—what is written about you. In other words, while academic rank is a factor influencing how letters of recommendation are perceived, the more critical factor is what the letter actually says about you. An outstanding letter from a junior faculty member that indicates that he or she knows you well and thinks highly of you is much better than a superficial letter from a senior faculty member.

Finally, remember that admissions committees will expect letters from certain faculty members. For example, if you completed an honors thesis, they will expect a letter from the faculty member who supervised your thesis.

WHO NOT TO ASK

Should you ask an employer for a letter of recommendation to graduate school? Only if your job was related to psychology and the letter discusses your duties and aptitude for this kind of work. Otherwise employers aren't good sources of letters. Don't ask relatives or friends of the family (even if they're doctors, lawyers, or political figures like mayors or senators) to write letters on your behalf. These letters, although well-intentioned, will not help your application because they do not comment on your ability as a researcher, student, or practitioner. In fact, they can sometimes hurt your application because they suggest that you don't understand the norms of academia and graduate education. Finally, never ask your therapist or psychologist to send a letter on your behalf.

Should you ever send more than the required number of recommendation letters? Only include an additional one or two letters *if* they provide information that isn't available in the other letters and thereby strengthen your application. Do not include additional letters if they are just lukewarm or are from irrelevant sources. If the extra letter truly adds something new and is very positive, then it could be helpful in your file, but be judicious in requesting additional letters of recommendation.

APPROACHING REFEREES

Remember that having someone write a letter of recommendation is a privilege, not a right. In other words, professors don't have to grant your request for a letter. Also, recommendation letters are difficult to write and professors are busy, so ask early and do what you can to make their task easier. Approach professors early, at least two months beforehand to request letters. As the end of the semester approaches, faculty may hesitate because of time constraints.

Approach potential referees at an appropriate time, such as during their office hours or a scheduled meeting. Don't ask in the hall or after class. Instead, visit office hours and explain the purpose for your visit. When you approach potential referees, ask if they know you well enough to write a meaningful letter. For example, explain that you're applying to graduate school, describe your career goals, and ask "Would you feel comfortable writing a letter of recommendation on my behalf?" Pay attention to their demeanor. If you sense reluctance, thank them and ask someone else. You need a positive letter, so don't be afraid to ask a professor whether he or she can write a favorable recommendation on your behalf. Sometimes professors agree half-heartedly—don't accept such letters, but don't insult the professor by refusing a letter either. How can you protect yourself in a sensitive situation? Talk to the professor first to request help in writing letters on your behalf, then tell him or her that you'll send or drop off the forms, and copies of your essays, transcript, and resume. This way you have time to think about the conversation afterward and decide whether you think the person will write a helpful letter. If not, send a short note to say that you will not need a recommendation after all and thank him or her.

WHAT IF YOU'VE BEEN OUT OF SCHOOL FOR A WHILE?

So what if a few years have passed since you graduated college and you haven't kept in contact with professors? That's a difficult dilemma, indeed. It may sound strange, but try contacting your professors. Believe it or not, most of us usually keep records on classes and students for a very long time. We're used to hearing from old students years after graduation. So although it may seem as if it's a long shot, it may not be as difficult as you think. If you've been out of school for a while, also have one recommendation letter from someone who knows you now in a professional capacity related to psychology. Perhaps an employer who can attest to your work habits? An alternative is to enroll in a graduate course (as a nonmatriculated, or non-degree-seeking student), perform well, and then ask the professor to write on your behalf.

PROVIDE YOUR REFEREES WITH INFORMATION

Make an appointment with faculty who will write your recommendation letters and discuss your goals and motivations for graduate work. The best thing that you can do to ensure that your letters cover all the bases is to provide your referees with all the necessary information. Don't assume that they will remember anything about you. (I know, you're quite memorable, but think about what it must be like to have 150 or more students each semester!) Make an appointment to speak with your letter writers. Give your letter writers plenty of time (about a month at minimum) so that they can write effective letters; don't rush them. Provide a file with all of your background information:

- transcript
- resume or vitae
- admissions essays
- courses you've taken with them
- research experiences
- internship and other applied experiences
- honor societies to which you belong
- awards you've won (and descriptions of the criteria for the award)

- work experience (including descriptions of what you've done in each job)
- professional goals
- due date for the application
- copy of the application recommendation forms

Request all of your letters at once and include all of the forms, envelopes, and postage needed–don't give professors information in a piecemeal fashion as it's sure to get lost or at least irritate them. Make sure that each piece of information and recommendation form/envelope is clearly labeled and includes the due date. Tell professors what you've included and remind them that if they need any additional information they can contact you (and include a detailed list of your contact information including phone numbers and email addresses). Include a pre-addressed envelope for each letter with postage affixed. Some graduate programs request that applicants include all the recommendation letters in individually sealed envelopes within the application itself. Understand that some professors will refuse to provide you with the letter (even in a sealed and signed envelope); instead, they may opt to send it directly to the admissions office themselves. If the graduate school letters must be returned to you in a sealed envelope, be sure to write your name and the school's name on the outside of each envelope. Make sure that the professor has signed across the seal of the envelope. If a professor decides to send the letter directly to the admissions office, provide him or her with a stamped and addressed postcard so that the school may notify you when the letter is received.

ABOUT CONFIDENTIALITY

All recommendation forms ask you to decide whether to waive or retain your rights to see each recommendation. As you decide whether to retain your rights, remember that confidential letters tend to carry more weight with admissions committees. Committees may hold the view that professors who write "open" letters may not feel free to give their honest opinion and may devalue such letters. In addition, many faculty will not write a recommendation letter unless it is confidential. Other faculty may send you a copy of each letter, even if it is confidential. If you are unsure of what to decide, discuss it with your referees.

HOW TO GET GOOD LETTERS OF RECOMMENDATION

So, how do you ensure that you'll have good letters of recommendation? Develop relationships with faculty early in your academic career. By developing professional relationships with faculty, you'll learn a lot and may get access to opportunities to conduct research, meet professionals who can help you to reach your goals (e.g., a professor in a graduate department to which you might apply), and other opportunities such as internships, summer positions, and teaching assistantships. "Getting to know faculty is easier said than done," you're probably thinking. Remember that professors are people too. Show a genuine interest in what they do and you'll find that the relationship develops itself.

Show Interest

Get to know the faculty who teach the classes that you like. How do you do this? Don't show up in their office simply hoping to make a good impression because professors are busy people who don't like to waste time. Instead, ask questions about the course content, try to start a discussion about some of the ideas that have been presented in class. Starting a dialogue with your professor creates a good impression, is fun for both of you, and is a great way to learn something new. Ask questions because you want answers rather than in an attempt to flatter a professor or achieve a hidden agenda. In short, show honest interest. If you're not interested in your professor's content area, then find another professor to make contact with.

Enroll in Classes that Get You Noticed

Try to take small classes that require written work so that you can develop your writing skills and allow your professor to get to know you better. Try to take more than one course with a professor so that he or she can get to know you over many courses and see your work patterns over time.

Participate in Class

This is especially important if you must enroll in large classes. Remember that your goal is to get the professor to see you as a bright and articulate student. Only participate if you are prepared to do so. In other words, do the reading prior to class and ask appropriate questions based on the lectures and readings with the goal of integrating the content. Aside from reading and reviewing your notes, how can you prepare to participate in class? Consider prior classes, the assigned readings, and the syllabus to identify what the class will focus on. Try to identify questions that will be asked in class. Consider applications of the content from the readings. What does it mean in "the real world"? Bring your own questions to class. Of course, don't go overboard and overparticipate as so-called "brown-nosing" is obvious to professors and students—and usually disliked by both. Exhibits 8 and 9 present behaviors that faculty admire and hate to see in class—be advised!

Get Research Experience

Research experience is critical to your graduate application—and it's a wonderful way to let professors get to know you. Approaching a professor to ask if you can get involved in their research can be scary and certainly requires initiative, but the rewards are well worth it. Tell professors that you're looking to become involved in research. Explain that you hope to work closely with someone on their research and if you're perceived well, word will get around. If you do well in your courses and present yourself as competent, motivated, and committed, you might even be approached by a professor who is looking for help with his or her research.

As you look for a mentor, remember that the most popular professors may have more students coming to them than they can work with. Look to faculty who are actively involved in research and whose interests parallel yours as much as possible. Visit during office hours to ask a question or two about graduate school or your career interests and get a feel for the professor's approachability. If he or she seems interested in discussing these express your desire to gain some experience in research. In the vast majority of cases, there is no pay involved for assisting professors with their research. Instead you'll get a free learning experience that will improve your skills and abilities as well as make you more appealing to graduate schools and employers. Finally, volunteer to work closely with a professor only if you have the time to commit. Remember that falling behind or dropping out will reflect negatively on you–more so than if you hadn't become involved at all.

What kinds of things will you do if you assist a faculty member with his or her research? Your tasks will vary by faculty member, project, and area of psychology. You might be involved in data collection by administering surveys or maintaining and operating lab equipment. You might code and enter data, make photocopies, or write literature reviews. Here are some of the general tasks that research assistants might perform (Landrum, Davis, & Landrum, 2000):

- Collect data by administering surveys, interviews, or running research protocols.
- Score, code, and enter data into a spreadsheet or statistical analysis program.
- Conduct general library research including literature searches using databases (e.g., PsychInfo, Social Sciences Citation Index), making copies of articles, and ordering unavailable articles and books through interlibrary loan.
- Assist the faculty member to develop new research ideas.
- Use computer skills such as word processing, spreadsheet, scheduling and statistical analysis programs.
- Assist in preparing submissions for local or regional conferences and, if accepted, work on poster or oral presentations for professional conferences.
- Assist faculty in preparing a manuscript to submit the results of your collaborative research to a scientific journal.

What do you get out of working with a faculty member on his or her research?

- The thrill of generating new knowledge
- Skills that aren't easily attained in the classroom
- Working one-on-one with a faculty member
- Exposure to methodological techniques that will be helpful in completing your senior thesis or later graduate work
- Practice in written and oral communication skills by preparing papers for submission to professional conferences and journals

- Developing a mentoring relationship with a faculty member
- Acquiring outstanding letters of recommendation
- Learn how to think, organize, and problem solve

There are a lot of benefits to assisting faculty with their research, but it's also a big commitment. You'll be given responsibility to ensure that specific tasks get done. The faculty member will count on you to get it done right. Your performance here can give faculty members lots of good things to write in letters of recommendation. If you complete tasks competently, you might be asked to take on more responsibility and you will earn excellent letters of recommendation. However, there is a positive payoff from conducting research with faculty only if you perform competent work consistently. If you don't take the commitment seriously, are unreliable, or make repeated mistakes, your relationship with the faculty member will suffer (as will your recommendation). If you decide to work with a faculty member on his or her research, treat it as a primary responsibility.

Remember that your professors are people too and it will be easier to establish professional relationships with them and earn excellent letters of recommendation. Although you might feel uncomfortable asking for letters of recommendation, understand that your professors have had to ask for recommendation letters themselves. They were once in your shoes and they've had to ask for recommendations to apply to graduate school, fellowships, faculty positions, and tenure.

Exhibit 8. Behaviors that Faculty Appreciate in Class (adapted from Kuther, 2003)

- Interest
- Attentiveness during lecture
- Participation in class discussions
- Ask thoughtful questions
- Rarely miss class
- Sit near front of class
- Smile and say hello before or after class
- Visit during office hours to discuss class material, ask questions, or seek assistance

Exhibit 9. What Not To Do: How To Irritate a Faculty Member (adapted from Kuther, 2003)

- Talk or pass notes during class
- Do homework or other non-class-related activities in class
- Pack up books and belongings before class is over
- Make papers look longer by adding blank pages, using large font, and wide margins
- Sit at the back of class when there are empty seats near the front
- Sleep in class
- Roll your eyes
- Be more focused on grades than learning
- Speak with the professor for the first time near the end of the semester, to ask for extra credit
- Repeatedly ask, "Is this going to be on the test?"
- Leave class early, for no apparent reason
- Take multiple make-up exams
- After arriving late or missing a class, asking "Did I miss anything?"
- Let your cell phone or pager ring in class

Exhibit 10. Tips from Graduate Students

- Get in touch with your professors early in the semester and your college years so that they have the chance to get to know you.
- Work with professors on their research and keep in touch with them. When it comes time to ask for letters, they'll remember you.
- Give your referees plenty of time. Meet with them to go over your materials and be sure to give them a copy of your personal statement and transcript, and discuss your career goals.
- Don't hound faculty, but politely keep track of whether your letters were completed.
- Form better relationships with professors during office hours, volunteer opportunities, community service, and so on. For example, I chose to do my college work study in the psychology department. All of the professors got to know my strong work ethic and knew me by name. If they know you and know that you want to go to graduate school, they'll let you know of opportunities, programs, and the like. Get involved in the psychology club and *Psi Chi*–faculty remember that stuff and include it in their letters.

- Ask professors if they are able to write you strong letters of recommendation. If they say no, ask what it would take for them to learn more about you.
- Make things as easy as possible for the people you ask. Get in touch with them a few months before you plan to ask for the letter (which should be about two months before you need it). You'll feel better asking for the letter if you have recently made contact with them to see how they are doing.
- Make sure that you've made a good impression on faculty you ask.
- Start early by building relationships with the people who would potentially write recommendation letters for you. Professors and supervisors can and will write better letters if they get to know you well. They will be invested in your success. Also, the work you do for and with these individuals should stand out. It's tough for someone to write a recommendation letter for you if they know you as someone who does only what is needed to get by.
- I simply contacted former professors and supervisors by telephone to ask if they would write letters on my behalf. I know this makes some people nervous, but writing letters of recommendation is part of these people's jobs so they probably won't be annoyed or surprised by your request. Also, if you are graduating college now and know you won't be applying to grad school for a few years, ask your professors before you leave if they would prefer to file a letter on your behalf with career services or if they would prefer you to contact them with a list of your recent accomplishments just prior to the time you will be applying to grad school. (The latter is the better option.)
- Get to know professors. Go to office hours, stay after class. Show interest in what your professors are working on. They're just like the rest of us and are thrilled when someone is interested in their passions.
- It is important to get letters of recommendation from people who know you well. There is no point in getting a letter from a well-known professor if they know little to nothing about you. I asked professors and/or graduate students who knew me from courses and labs I worked at as a research assistant. Most of the people knew me for at least two or more years.

Chapter 8

I'VE SUBMITTED MY APPLICATION: NOW WHAT?

You've submitted your application. It's a momentous task. Though you may not feel like celebrating, submitting your application is a great deal of work and you deserve a reward. Have some fun, read a good book, and go out with your friends. Of course, most applicants find it difficult to keep from thinking about their applications after sending them in to the various graduate programs. In this chapter we'll talk about what happens to applications once they reach graduate admissions offices and how to manage the interminable waiting.

WHAT TO EXPECT

Expect to hear nothing, other than receive a postcard indicating that your application is complete. The wait will feel very long. What's happening to your application while you wait? The exact process varies by school and by department, but, generally, here's what happens:

- Applications are opened and filed.
- As each recommendation letter, transcript, or other component of an application arrives, it goes into the applicant's file.
- When a file is complete, it is screened.
- Screened files are typically divided into three groups: Excellent, Acceptable, and Unacceptable.
- Some, though not all, programs immediately send rejection letters to the applicants whose files were categorized as unacceptable.

- The admissions committee takes a closer look at the remaining files, comparing GRE scores, transcripts, letters of recommendation, and personal statements.
- Based on the comparisons as well as faculty members' interest in working with each applicant, a list of finalists is selected.
- If interviews are to occur, then the finalists are invited to campus.
- If no interviews occur, the finalists are sent acceptance letters. Typically rejections are sent at this point (though some programs instead wait until the very end of the application season, after all offers of admission have been accepted).
- A backup list of acceptable candidates usually is kept in reserve because many of the top candidates may accept offers at other schools.
- As candidates decline offers, additional letters of acceptance are sent to remaining acceptable candidates.
- The process ends in mid April, when applicants must inform programs of their intent to accept or decline an offer.
- Occasionally an acceptance is sent out later after receiving a candidate's decline.

SHOULD YOU MAKE CONTACT?

Waiting is hard to deal with because at this point in the application process, you have no control. Lots of students become impatient and wonder whether they should contact the admissions office or call faculty to learn about their status. Beware! One of the biggest pet peeves faculty and admissions offices have are applicants who make contact too frequently. So, before you pick up that phone or send that email, carefully consider why you're making contact, if it's reasonable, and how it's likely to be perceived.

When to Make Contact

There is one time when you shouldn't hesitate to make contact: when you haven't received a confirmation that your application is complete. Frequently graduate programs will send postcards to notify applicants that their files are complete or that they're missing an item.

Some programs don't notify applicants of missing materials and sometimes applicants learn of missing materials only after being rejected from a graduate program. Unfortunately, sometimes applications are dropped from consideration because of missing materials and applicants aren't notified, as in the case of one of my students whose transcript was not received in time. If you have not received a postcard by two to three weeks after you've sent your application (be sure to send it early so that you don't go over the admissions deadline if additional materials arrive late), call the admissions office to ensure that your file is complete. Remember to be polite and cordial because you don't know who will answer the phone and an impolite applicant may be fast-tracked a rejection letter. Better yet, send an email instead.

Another time to make contact is when part of your application changes, for example, if you're awarded a prestigious fellowship, or if a paper is accepted for presentation at a conference or publication in a journal. If you're fortunate enough to experience events that improve your application, send a follow-up letter notifying the admissions committee of your success and asking that the update be included in your file. Because you don't know the timing of admissions decisions, it's a good idea to fax the letter and send a hard copy as a follow-up so that the committee gets updated information immediately.

Finally, consider calling if the published decision date has passed and you haven't heard anything. A quick call to inquire about the timetable for decisions is appropriate if the decision date has passed. Also, if you've been accepted to a program and are waiting to hear about other applications, it's entirely appropriate to contact the programs, explain that you've been accepted but are still interested in the program and would like to know when decisions will be made.

When Not to Make Contact

Don't make contact out of nervousness or because you can't stand the wait. Sure, if you call repeatedly or send a few emails, your name will get noticed, but not for the right reasons! Keith-Speigel and Weiderman (2000) report that applicants often contact departments for the wrong reasons, such as inquiring about their status a week after applications are due, requesting an interview to discuss their status, having someone else call to get feedback about their application, or calling to ask about the quality of the other applications. Even worse, these contacts are often made with a rude demeanor. Don't let yourself become one of these dreaded applicants!

Remember that there is a lot of competition among graduate schools for good students, so admissions committees work as fast as they can because they don't want to lose their best applicants. The reality is that the process is lengthy and takes a lot of hard work and time on the part of the admissions committee. Committees try to make decisions as early as possible and contact successful applicants immediately. So have faith, you will hear back.

WAITING: WHAT TO DO NOW?

The good part of having turned in your applications is that you have nothing left to do—all the hard work is done. The bad part, of course, is that you have nothing to do—nothing to occupy yourself as you wait for news about your application. Waiting stinks. What can you do to ease the pain?

- Try to forget about your application. I know, easier said than done. Have some fun and enjoy your last semester in college.
- Make a back-up plan so that you feel that you have something to fall back on. Consider what you would do if you didn't get into your top choice. Evaluate your credentials and decide how to improve them, if needed.
- Master's programs accept applications later, usually, so you could apply to a few if you're really antsy and concerned.
- Do well in class, work on finishing up your requirements for graduation.
- Research the faculty. Sure, you looked into each program's faculty, as well as faculty members' research interests, when you were deciding where to submit your applications, but now you have time to learn more as well as prepare for possible interviews.
- Take time for yourself. Remember that if you get into a graduate program, the next few years will be very busy, so take time now to do things you enjoy. Waiting is difficult, but before you know it, you'll begin to hear back from programs.

HEARING BACK

There's no way to know when you'll hear back from the graduate schools to which you've applied. Although they must notify you by April 15, some programs notify their best applicants shortly after the application deadline has passed and others take months. One thing is certain: When you finally do hear, you'll be surprised. You may also be surprised by how a graduate program contacts you. You might receive word of acceptance by phone, email, or mail–though in recent years it seems that phone calls and email are the methods of choice given graduate programs' desires to lure the best students. Rejection letters, however, haven't changed: they arrive in a business-sized envelope on a single piece of paper.

Some, though not all, schools may contact you to arrange a phone or in-person interview. In Chapter 9 we discuss the interview in detail, but for now remember that if a member of a graduate admissions committee calls you for a phone interview and asks you to answer a few questions immediately, explain that you were just on your way out and arrange a later time to talk. No matter how excited you are, don't speak to him or her immediately. The extra time, even if it's just an hour or two, will allow you to refresh your memory about the program, consider your responses to common interview questions, and review the interview tips that we'll discuss in the next chapter.

Exhibit 11. Tips from Graduate Students

- After you turn in your application, you've done your part. If you've done all you could do to prepare a good application, then you should sit back and relax. It's out of your hands at that point. I think it's sometimes more anxiety-provoking to have to decide between two or more schools than to wait for their responses. Regardless of the outcome, you should be proud of the fact that you've "survived" through the whole application process.
- Let it go–it's out of your hands. Just trust that life has a way of working out the way it's supposed to. You work hard to put yourself in the best spot possible–the rest takes care of itself.

- Hard as it is, relax and work on a hobby. Tension builds and tempers flare as the days pass and the waiting seems to endure forever. Maintain your confidence.
- There's absolutely nothing you can do to change the process. Don't think about it. Find something else to concentrate on, like graduation.
- Immerse yourself in a hobby or job unrelated to psychology. The less you are reminded about psychology in general, the better. Read that book for pleasure, the one that you haven't had time to sit down with. Go rent those movies you wanted to see but didn't because you had to work on your personal statement instead. Distance yourself from the world of psychology a bit–when applying it's all that you eat, sleep, and breathe–make a conscious effort to get away.

Chapter 9

THE INTERVIEW

While interviews aren't a required component for all graduate programs, be prepared for the possibility, especially if you're applying to clinical or counseling psychology programs as well programs in other applied areas of psychology. As admission to graduate school becomes more competitive, admissions interviews are becoming commonplace across the subdisciplines of psychology. If you're invited for an interview, rest assured that you've made it to the short list of finalists. Interviews are time consuming and expensive, so only finalists in the application process are invited. However, also remember that more applicants are invited than can be accepted, so your performance is critical.

PURPOSE OF THE INTERVIEW

The interview provides the graduate admissions committee with an opportunity to meet you, the person, apart from your written application. They'll get to learn about you as an individual and to determine whether you have what it takes to succeed in graduate school and the profession, like maturity, interpersonal skills, interest, and motivation. Your personal characteristics, personality, and interpersonal skills are especially important to your application to clinical psychology programs or other applied "people-oriented" programs. The admissions committee will evaluate how well you express yourself, manage stress, and think on your feet.

Once you get into graduate school, you'll work very closely with a faculty member for several years. It's no wonder, then, that professors want to meet potential students—and you should meet them too. Do you really want to commit to working with a faculty member for the foreseeable future, without meeting him or her beforehand? The interview offers you an opportunity to learn about the school, program, faculty, and students to determine if it's the right match for you. During the interview, you should be evaluating the program just as they are evaluating you. Later in this chapter we'll talk about questions to ask and things to look for during your interview.

WHAT TO EXPECT

Interview formats vary considerably. Some programs don't do interviews at all. Others conduct interviews by telephone. Some programs will request applicants to meet for half of an hour to an hour with a faculty member; other interviews will be full weekend events with students, faculty, and other applicants. Graduate school interviews are conducted by invitation but the expenses are nearly always paid for by applicants. In some unusual cases a program may assist a promising student with travel expenses, but it's not common. If you're invited to an interview, be sure to attend even if you have to pay the travel expenses. Not attending, even if it's for a good reason, signals that you're not seriously interested in the program.

During your interview you'll have the opportunity to talk with several faculty members as well as students. You might engage in small group discussions with students, faculty, and other applicants. Be sure to participate in discussions, demonstrate your listening skills, and not monopolize the conversation. During your interviews, the interviewers may have read your application file, but don't expect them to remember anything about you. Because the interviewer is unlikely to remember much about each applicant, be forthcoming about your experiences, strengths, and professional goals. Be mindful of the salient facts you wish to present.

PREPARING FOR THE INTERVIEW

How do you prepare for this mammoth event? Prepare as if it were a job interview. In essence, it is. If accepted, your job for the next few years will be "student."

- Do your homework. Learn about the program and faculty. Read recent faculty publications to learn more about their research. Understand the training emphasis.
- Review your own interests, goals, and qualifications. Note what things make you a good match for the program. Be able to explain how your goals and qualifications match what the program has to offer.
- Take the perspective of faculty members. What can you contribute to their graduate program and research? Why should they accept you? What skills do you bring that will help a professor advance in his or her research?
- Anticipate questions and rehearse potential answers (see the list of possible questions later in the next section).
- Conduct a mock interview with a friend or family member. Encourage them to tell you about any distracting nonverbal behavior (like touching your hair, clenching your hands, or using your hands too flamboyantly). Also practice in front of a mirror.
- Prepare intelligent questions to ask. Remember that you're judged by your application but also by your presentation and your interest in the program and faculty. Later in this chapter we'll talk about potential questions to ask during your interview.
- What should you wear? Dress professionally and comfortably. Both men and women should wear suits, or jacket and pants/skirt combinations. Pay attention to detail: polish your shoes, clean and well kept (subtle) nails, minimal makeup and cologne/perfume, minimal jewelry.

DURING THE INTERVIEW

Remember your goals during your interview: to convey your interest, motivation, and professionalism, and to gather the information you need to determine if this is the graduate program for you.

- In meetings with graduate students, try to ask questions to learn what they really think about their advisors and the program. Most students will be forthcoming–especially in one-on-one conversations.

- Don't underestimate the potential influence of current graduate students. Although they might sound like they're speaking off-the-cuff, remember that you're on an interview, regardless of with whom you're speaking. Present your best side because current graduate students may be in a position to help or hurt your application.
- Follow standard rules of interviewing (i.e., eye contact, self-confident presentation, conservative dress, etc.). More tips on the "rules of interviewing" appear later in this chapter.
- Some interviews include social events like parties. Don't drink too much (even if others do). Remember that even though it seems like a party, it's an interview. Assume that you're being evaluated at all times.

Common Interview Questions

While you cannot predict everything about your interview–much will vary based on the program and faculty involved–you can predict at least some of the questions you're likely to be asked. Here are some of the most common interview questions. Don't prepare written answers or memorize answers (you'll appear too stiff). Instead consider your responses to each and be prepared to talk extemporaneously about each.

- Tell me about yourself.
- What are your career goals?
- Why psychology?
- Tell me about your strengths and weaknesses.
- Why would you be an asset to our department?
- What kind of teaching experiences have you had?
- What kind of research experiences have you had?
- Why should we accept you into this program?
- Why are you suited for a career in psychology?
- What appeals to you about our program?
- To what other schools are you applying?
- Tell me about the research project you were involved in during college.
- What events have led to your desire to become a psychologist? What experiences and people influenced your decision?

- In what extracurricular activities have you been involved? What role(s) did you play? How did you grow through the experience?
- How do you view the future of clinical (or other subdiscipline of) psychology?
- How are you unique? What and how do you expect to contribute to the profession?
- How will you contribute to our program?
- In what type of setting would you like to practice, work, or teach?
- Explain your lowest test score.
- What is your theoretical orientation? Your research orientation? Applied orientation?
- What are your outside interests? Have any talents (e.g., music, art, etc.)?
- What are your favorite reading materials, music, films?
-   Are you a well-rounded person? Explain.
- How have you gotten involved in community service?
- How do you deal with stress?
- What will you do career-wise if not admitted to this professional graduate school program?
- How do you plan to finance your graduate education?
- How do you deal with uncertainty or failure? Provide an example from your life. What did you learn?
- How would family, friends, and teachers describe you?
- What do you think it takes to be successful in psychology?
- Why do you want to be a clinical psychologist? What qualifications do you have that will make you a successful psychologist?
- Have you ever had personal therapy? If yes, what sort of issues did you work on? If no, why not?
- What are your research interests? Tell me about your research project/honors thesis or independent study.
- What is your theoretical orientation?
- Which of our faculty members do you think you would work with? Why?
- Where else have you applied or interviewed?
- In what area would you like to conduct research?
- If you were to devise a research project right this moment, what would be the topic? Tell me about it.
- What do you know about our program?
- What are your strengths and weaknesses with regard to research?

- Which undergraduate course did you like best? Why?
- Which course did you like least? Why?

Consider your responses to each of these questions, but don't memorize answers. Focus on expressing yourself in a concise way that highlights your strengths. What's unique about your experience that will make you memorable? Your goal is to engage the interviewer in conversation, not lecture to him or her. If you memorize answers, you'll appear stiff and won't convey your interest and motivation. Throughout, emphasize what you have to offer to the program and the profession, not what they have to offer you or what you'll get out of it. Whatever you do, be honest and be yourself. Do not make up answers or give the interviewer what you think he or she wants to hear. It's obvious and will backfire.

What to Ask

During your interview, you'll be judged on your responses to questions, but also on what questions you ask. Carefully study the materials that you've gathered about the program and faculty before your interview so that you can devise questions that will provide you with the information you need to make an educated decision—and will impress your interviewers. Use the interview as your opportunity to learn more about the school and understand the subtle differences among programs. However, be sure to do your homework beforehand. Your questions should reflect your research about the program and school. Beginner's-level questions will be more harmful than helpful as low-level questions indicate a lack of interest and initiative. Ask similar questions of all with whom you interview so that you can get a range of perspectives (i.e., different people may provide different responses to your questions).

Your questions reveal information about your interest in the program, your personality, interpersonal skills, motivation, and reasoning skills. What should you ask? Of course, you need to determine what questions are of interest to you and appropriate to the program, but here are some samples to get you started. Write down your list of questions. It's ok to ask to refer back to your list so that you don't forget anything. In fact, it can often impress your interviewer that you've considered the program seriously and planned your questions so carefully. If you have no questions to ask, you may be perceived as uninterested, passive, and even boring.

- In your view, what are the most distinguishing characteristics of this program?
- Where are recent alumni employed? What do most students do after graduation?
- What types of financial aid are offered? What criteria are used for choosing recipients?
- Are there any scholarships or fellowships available? How do I apply?
- Are there teaching opportunities, such as teaching assistantships and adjunct positions, for current students?
- Do most students publish an article or present a paper before graduation?
- What planned practical experiences are included in the program (e.g., internships)? Ask for examples of internship placements.
- What is the relative importance of admissions test scores, undergraduate grades, recommendations, statements on applications, experience, and other requirements?
- If you could change any feature about your program or school, what would it be?
- How would you characterize the interaction between professors and students?
- How well do students get along? Would you describe the atmosphere as cooperative or competitive?
- What kind of career counseling is available to students? Are there campus resources available to help students obtain jobs after graduation?
- What is the typical program of study? What courses are required?
- Are their opportunities to tailor the program of study based on a student's interests (e.g., to include additional courses in social policy or law?)
- How long does it take the typical student to complete this program?
- I've read articles written by _____, _____, and _____. To what extent are students involved in assisting them with their research projects?
- When are comprehensive exams taken?

Interviewing Tips

- Remember your manners.
- Be early, if possible. If you're traveling a distance (e.g., traveling by air or more than a few hours by car), arrive the day before to ensure that you have time to relax, rest, and be on time.
- Try to relax (relaxation tips appear at the end of this chapter).
- Drink plenty of water before and during the interview to keep yourself hydrated and your thoughts clear.
- Be friendly. Greet and shake hands with the interviewer (firm handshake, not a limp fish!) and repeat the interviewer's name ("Nice to meet you, Dr. Jones").
- Make good eye contact.
- Lean toward an interviewer to show interest and enthusiasm.
- Listen carefully and attempt to answer each question posed. If you don't understand a question, ask for clarification.
- If an interviewer challenges you, be flexible and adaptive. Respect the interviewer's point of view, but don't change your opinions to please him or her.
- Avoid sounding rehearsed.
- Be serious, but try to let your enthusiasm and motivation show in your responses and your smile.
- Remember to turn off your cell phone or pager before the interview. If your phone rings, silence it and do not answer it.
- Engage in conversation with your interviewer, relying on your preparation beforehand to guide you.
- Pay attention to your nonverbal behavior. Be aware of any facial expressions and body movements that can work against the image you're attempting to present.
- Don't criticize your university, department, or professors. Sometimes applicants are encouraged to vent. Committee members may use this as an opportunity to learn about your maturity.
- Don't hang out your dirty laundry. Don't bare your soul, talk about personal matters (like your history of mental health or that of your family members or friends).
- Be positive. Remember that whenever you speak negatively about another person or situation you run the risk of appearing like a troubled person who may have difficulty working with others. That's not the image you want to present.

- Be honest. Follow up questions will reveal if you've stretched the truth. If you don't understand a question, ask for an explanation. Don't just fake it because it will be obvious to the interviewer.
- Don't rush to answer questions. Whenever you are asked a question, wait a moment to consider it rather than responding right away. Focus on speaking slowly, addressing the question at hand, being complete in your answer, and not straying from the topic.

Managing Social Situations

Sometimes graduate admissions interviews include social events like dinners and parties. It might seem like the right time to let down your guard, but remember that you're still on an interview. What's the purpose of these events? They're not meant to make you feel uncomfortable. Instead, social activities let applicants, graduate students, and faculty get to know each other better. Once you enter a graduate program, you'll work very closely with faculty members and students for a long time, so it's important to be able to get along. Social events let professors see how well you'll fit in. So, relax a little while keeping in mind that it is still an interview. The conversation might focus on research or it might be on the light side. Either way, take your host's cues as to what to talk about. If you're asked any formal questions, try to answer them as best you can. Always remember that your conversations may be shared with others and used to determine your appropriateness for the program. For that reason, you're better off not drinking any alcoholic beverages or consuming one drink at most because you'll need to keep your faculties about you.

STRESS MANAGEMENT: COPING WITH THE INTERVIEW

Some nervousness is to be expected. The more prepared you are the better you'll feel, so consider possible questions and your responses, and enlist friends and family for mock interviews. Practice relaxation techniques before your interview so that you'll be well versed in how to cool down when the pressure hits.

- Practice deep breathing. Sit up with your back straight. Place one hand on your abdomen and the other on your chest. Breathe in through your nose. As you inhale, your abdomen should begin to rise, but your chest should move very little. Exhale and contract your abdominal muscles releasing as much air as possible. It takes time for abdominal breathing to become automatic and natural for you, so practice it often.
- Practice progressive muscle relaxation, in which you repeatedly tense and release muscles to promote relaxation. Close your eyes. Tighten your face. Hold for a five seconds. Relax. Repeat. Do the same for your jaw. Then your lips. Raise your shoulders and hold for five seconds, release, and repeat. Tighten your arms and fists and hold, relax, and repeat. Then your stomach, buttocks, thighs, calves, and feet. Then move back up your body, tightening each part and releasing. Notice how loose your muscles are. Breathe deeply and open your eyes.
- Make a conscious effort to relax your neck and shoulders by rolling your neck, pulling your shoulders up to your ears and back, and rolling your shoulders.
- Practice positive self-talk. Remind yourself of your strengths. Feel good about yourself because if you've prepared well, there is no need to feel nervous.
- Take a moment before you respond to each question posed to you. Breathe in deeply through your nose and exhale all the way before beginning your answer. The extra moment of thinking time is useful and will help you to feel more calm and controlled.
- Remember to smile—it's a tension reliever.
- Understand that some anxiety is a normal part of facing a challenge like an interview. A little bit of anxiety can even help you by keeping you on your toes and making you a little sharper. Use it as an energy enhancer to uplift your performance.
- Keep in mind that the admissions committee wants you to succeed. They want to help you to bring out your best because they want to see you as you truly are.
- The admissions committee is sympathetic to signs of nerves. They understand that you're likely to feel stressed.
- Remember that anxiety is felt rather than seen—we feel worse than we look.

AFTER THE INTERVIEW

After the interview, the period of waiting returns. You will be tempted to obsess over the interview, try to decipher the interviewer's cues, and rethink your responses.

- Try to keep a balanced view of your performance. Evaluate yourself constructively. Make an effort to notice and congratulate yourself on the things you think you did well, not just what you didn't like.
- If you must criticize yourself, be specific. Specific criticism, spelling out where you can improve, will enhance your performance next time.
- Take time to pamper yourself. You deserve a reward for making it through such a challenging experience—no matter the outcome.

Try not to obsess because there is nothing that you can do now. You prepared and gave it your all. Now you must wait.

Should you send a thank-you note? Though a thank-you note is generally thoughtful, it's difficult to predict how it will be viewed. If the committee went out of their way for applicants (e.g., an expensive dinner, a big social party, or a long tour of the university and surrounding area) you might consider sending a brief thank-you note to the group as a whole. If you stayed with a graduate student, consider sending him or her a note. If you decide to send a thank-you note, make it short and be sure that it is a thank-you note. Offer your gratitude, but don't take it as an opportunity to discuss your candidacy or your note may be perceived as manipulative.

Exhibit 12. Tips from Graduate Students

- My graduate program did not require an interview. However, I flew out to the campus and did an "interview" anyway even though I was already accepted. It is important to visit the department and meet the faculty and students. You can get a lot of important information by talking to the people there. Talking to the current graduate students there also gives you a good idea of what your life might be like if you attended that program. Even if interviews are not required, be sure to visit the program and talk to the people there.

- Read up on the faculty who you will be interviewing with. This will help you to identify areas in which you might have similarities and whether you'll be a good fit. Don't act like you know everything about them in the interview.
- Be early. Be inquisitive and have a practice interview first.
- Take the time to learn about the program and school. Don't get so caught up in the interview that you forget to ask the questions that will help you to get the information you need to decide among schools. Ask the tough questions about expectations, assistantships, access to faculty, etc.
- Be ready for questions about your research interests. Remember what you said in your personal statement. Be nice. Ask questions, like what is the area like, or what is the general amount of time it takes to complete this program, or what are some of the centers, schools, etc. nearby and is the school able to "use" them for research purposes.
- Dress professionally, regardless of what you think you can get away with on an interview. Know your audience. Learn everyone's name and interests before you arrive. Be nice to the graduate students–you would be surprised by the amount of influence that they have. Be yourself. If you fake it during the interview, you will not really know if you fit in for the five-plus year stretch. Go to all the in-person interviews you can. Even if you think that you won't want to attend, it is a great learning experience. I learned a lot.
- For clinical programs, there are often two primary purposes to the interview, which are highly related. The first is to assess whether you have the communication skills/personality characteristics necessary to work with people clinically. The second is to determine whether you would be a good "fit" with the other students and the faculty in the department. So mostly, trite as it sounds, try to be yourself. I really enjoy interviewing people who seem genuine. Be respectful, but there is no need to get anxious over every aspect of your behavior. I've noticed that interviewees become very nervous and seem to think that everything about them is going to offend the interviewers. I had one interviewee apologize profusely because she thought she took too much soda! That said, know your work you have been doing well and be able to talk about it intelligently.

- Be prepared. Know something about the program you're visiting, the professors who work there, etc. Also, have a clear message to give interviewers about your own qualifications, interests, and degree of flexibility. Most importantly, be polite and not arrogant. While it is important to sell yourself in an interview, it's more important to show that you're someone who would make a good colleague.
- Know what your strong points are and be prepared to talk about them; work them into the interview in some way so that you can toot your own horn. This may feel uncomfortable, but the interview is your time to show a program all the good things that you've done and will continue to do should you be accepted. But be careful to think about exactly what message you want to send when you talk about yourself.
- Prepare good and thought-provoking questions. They don't have to be about your interviewer's particular area of interest, but about the program itself. As a student interviewer, I am always more impressed by an applicant that poses a thought-provoking question than one who asks the standard stuff.

Chapter 10

DECISION TIME

The waiting is finally over. Congratulations! You've been accepted by one or more programs! Though choosing schools to which to apply and preparing each application was difficult, your next challenge might seem especially harrowing. How do you choose which program to attend? Go back to your notes from Chapter 2. What are your goals and what are your priorities? Use what you've learned about yourself to weigh the various programs and make a decision of where to attend graduate school.

EVALUATING OFFERS AND GRADUATE PROGRAMS

What should you consider in evaluating programs? We've discussed indicators of quality, but to summarize, consider the following:

- What is the program's educational philosophy?
- What are the training emphases?
- How are graduates employed?
- Who are the faculty and how well known are they?
- Do faculty work closely with students?
- How large is the program? How many students are enrolled?
- How frequently do the faculty publish?
- What kinds of funding have you been awarded?
- What other sources of financial aid are available?
- Does one program offer especially unique classes?

Also remember that you're making a decision about a major life change. You're choosing a new place to live. Consider the geographic location. Will you feel comfortable living there for several years? What's the cost of living? Remember that the cost of living varies widely across the country. A $15,000 stipend might seem like a lot, but it will get you much further in Bloomington, Indiana than in New York City. Can you manage on the funding provided or will you need additional financial assistance?

Don't limit your research to the Internet and brochures. Contact faculty and graduate students at each program to which you've been accepted. Gather information from various sources to piece together a complete picture about each program. Do the graduate students feel valued? Do they have adequate opportunities for research? Do they publish articles and present papers with faculty? Do they get teaching experience? Do they have many job opportunities available to them after graduation? You might get different responses to each of these questions from graduate students, faculty, and recent graduates. Make a list of all of the positive and negative features of each program and use your lists to rank the programs to which you've been accepted. If you're still finding choosing a program difficult, solicit input from your professors (but don't rely too much on their input as where to attend graduate school is your choice and must be your decision).

NOTIFYING GRADUATE PROGRAMS

Remember that other applicants are waiting to hear from graduate programs and the longer that you wait before letting a program know that you're not interested in attending, the longer other applicants must wait to get their acceptance letters. Be considerate of others. As soon as you have two offers, decide which is better and notify the other program that you're declining their offer of admission. Repeat this comparison process as you receive each new offer. Admissions committees will appreciate your timeliness and honesty—and they will be able to move on to the next candidate on their list. You hurt other candidates, your peers, by holding on to offers that you have no intention of accepting. Notify programs as soon as you realize that you'll decline their offer.

How do you decline an offer of admission? Send a short email or fax a letter thanking them for the offer and notifying them of your decision. Address the note to your contact person or to the entire graduate admissions committee, and simply explain your decision. For example:

I am writing in response to your offer of admission to the Clinical Psychology program at Graduate University. I appreciate your interest in me, but I regret to inform you that I will not be accepting your offer of admission. Thank you for your time and consideration.

Be sure to type your name and then sign the letter. You may notify the program by email, fax, or phone, but be sure to follow up with a written letter because messages are sometimes lost.

You may find that some programs may pressure you to make a decision and accept their offer of admission before April 15. It's not appropriate for the committee to pressure you, so stand your ground (unless you're absolutely certain that it is the program for you). Remember that you're not obligated to make a decision until April 15. When you've accepted an offer of admission, remember that you are committed to that acceptance. If you attempt to be released from an acceptance agreement, you might make waves and gain an unsavory reputation among graduate programs in psychology (it's a very small world indeed) and among the faculty who have provided you with letters of recommendation.

When you're ready to accept an offer of admission, call or email your contact for the program and follow up with a written letter that is faxed and then mailed to the program. A short professional looking note indicating that you've made your decision and are pleased to accept their offer of admission is adequate. For example:

Dear Dr. Smith (or Admissions Committee)

I am writing to notify you of my decision to accept your offer to enroll in the Clinical Psychology program at Graduate University. Thank you for your time and consideration. I look forward to attending your program this Fall and am excited by the opportunities that await.

Of course, tailor the letter to your own style and needs. Be sure to sign the letter above your typed name (to ensure that they know the letter is from you!). Congratulations on completing a milestone in your life.

BEING WAIT-LISTED

Graduate admissions committees realize that not all candidates who are accepted will take them up on their offer of admission. Sometimes admissions committees don't notify the candidates they've selected as alternates; they wait and notify them of acceptance if a slot opens rather than telling candidates that they've been wait-listed (and perhaps getting candidates' hopes up prematurely). More frequently, applicants who are alternates are sent letters indicating their alternate or wait-list status. If you're wait-listed, then you're waiting to see if a slot opens—if a candidate who has been offered admission declines.

What do you do if you're an alternate? Wait. Take the time to consider whether the program is still of interest to you. If you've been accepted elsewhere and plan to attend, notify the admissions committee to withdraw yourself from the wait-list. If you receive an offer from another program but you're more interested in the program to which you're an alternate, it's permissible to follow up and inquire if any more information is available if the April 15 deadline is approaching. Understand that the program staff may not have more information, but, like you, they want to end the process as quickly as possible. If you're down to the wire and have an offer of admission, sometimes you'll have to make a decision to withdraw your alternate status or run the risk of declining a solid offer of admission for something that may never materialize (forcing you to start the graduate admissions process all over again).

REJECTION

You followed all the directions, prepared for the GRE, obtained excellent recommendations and still received a rejection letter. What gives? It's difficult to learn that you're not among a program's top choices—especially after investing so much time and effort. From a statistical standpoint, you have lots of company; many doctoral programs in psychology receive ten to 50 times as many applicants than they can take. Understand that under these circumstances many are excellent and only a hair different from those that are accepted. That probably doesn't make you feel any better, though. It may be particularly difficult if you were invited for an interview; however, as many as 75% of applicants invited for interviews are not accepted.

Why Are Students Rejected?

There simply aren't enough slots. Most graduate programs receive far more applications from qualified candidates than they can accept. Why were you eliminated by a particular program? There is no way to tell, but in many cases applicants are rejected because they demonstrated poor "fit." In other words, their interests and career aspirations didn't fit the program. For example, an applicant to a research-oriented clinical psychology program who didn't read the program materials carefully might be rejected for indicating an interest in practicing therapy. If you are rejected to every program to which you apply, reassess your goals, but don't necessarily give up. Ask yourself some hard questions and try your best to answer them honestly:

- Did you select schools carefully, paying attention to fit?
- Did you apply to enough programs?
- Did you complete all parts of each application?
- Did you spend enough time on your essays?
- Did you tailor your essays to each program?
- Did you have research experience?
- Did you have field or applied experience?
- Did you know your referees well and did they have something to write about?
- Were most of your applications to highly competitive programs?

Your answers to these questions may help you determine whether to reapply next year, apply to a master's program instead, or choose another career path. If you are firmly committed to attending graduate school, consider reapplying next year. Also remember that if you receive no offers by April 15, there's still a small possibility that you may be admitted at a later time. The APA Education Directorate publishes a list of remaining openings in May (the list can be found on the APA website, http://www.apa.org).

How to Proceed After Rejection

After receiving word of rejection from the graduate programs to which you've applied, your first step should be to seek social support. You might find it difficult to inform family, friends, and professors of the bad news, but it is essential that you seek social support. Allow yourself to feel upset and acknowledge your feelings, then move forward. What are your options? You can apply to a master's program immediately, reapply next year, or choose another career path.

Apply to a Master's Program

Consider immediately applying to a master's program if you suspect that you're not ready for a doctoral program. If you decide to go the master's route, you must decide what sort of master's program to attend. Some students may decide that a master's degree offers all the preparation they need for the careers they desire. In some states, for example, graduates with master's degrees in psychology can be licensed as counselors (Kuther, 2003). Other students may choose a master's program as a stepping stone towards a doctoral program. If this is true of you, consider a research-oriented master's program such as in experimental or quantitative psychology in order to develop and demonstrate your propensity for undertaking research. Seek additional research experiences, presentation and publication opportunities, and, if you're interested in clinical or counseling psychology, applied experiences to strengthen your application to doctoral programs.

Reapply Next Year

Many students decide to reapply to graduate school the following year after evaluating their applications and creating a plan to improve their credentials. Review the suggestions in Chapter 3. Work on improving your academic record, perhaps by taking additional courses in math and science, or by taking a nonmatriculated graduate course (i.e., one without being formally enrolled in a graduate program) at your university. Seek research experience and keep in contact with your professors. If your GRE scores are on the low end, consider enrolling in a preparation course and retaking them (only if you're committed and believe that you can make a major improvement in your score).

Stay focused. If you plan on applying to graduate school again next year, create a plan now. Map out the upcoming months to ensure that you'll keep on track, not waste time, and obtain the experiences that you need to be more marketable to graduate programs. Sometimes students forget to reapply to graduate school, or remember at the last minute. Don't end up in that position. Use a calendar to keep track of what you're doing and when to reapply to graduate school.

Next time around, apply to a wider range of schools (including "safety" schools), select programs more carefully, and thoroughly research and tailor your application to each program. If you're applying to some of the same programs that rejected you, be sure that you've improved your credentials in the interim as admissions committees may examine a second application for significant change. If you work at improving your credentials, you may be admitted to a graduate program this time—it happens quite often.

Consider Your Career Path

Sometimes when students are rejected from the graduate programs to which they've applied they reconsider their career goals all together. You may be uncertain of the choices you've made. That's normal. Seek career counseling. Several books on the market offer assistance in evaluating interests, values, and personality characteristics and helping readers to choose careers. Check the resources listed in the appendix of this book to help you to find your career path and determine whether a change in your career goals is needed.

Exhibit 13. Tips Advice from Graduate Students

- I had to apply three times and the third time was the charm. Never give up if you know that's what you want to do. If you are rejected, make sure you learn from the experience and find ways to improve your application for the next time. Being rejected doesn't mean that you aren't a qualified candidate or that you were not meant to go to graduate school. There are many reasons why programs reject candidates. So find out how to improve your application and find the right match for you.
- If you're rejected, try again. Contact each program and find out your status and why they rejected you. The feedback can be invaluable. Also, be sure that you don't burn any bridges.
- If you diversify your applications with low, medium, and high difficulty programs, you should get offered something.

- If you're rejected from a clinical psychology program, consider related careers of interest that might be less competitive than clinical psychology programs that only let a few students in each year.
- Being rejected is not the end of the world. Work on either raising your GRE scores (if they were low), or working in either a clinical or lab setting to gain more experience and possibly get stronger letters of recommendation. Think really hard if grad school is something that you truly want to work for. Also, consider a master's program. Sometimes the deadlines are later.
- I didn't get in the first year I applied. So I worked for a year, I did more research about other programs I wanted to apply to, and I re-applied the following year. Now, I am in a program that I absolutely love and I couldn't imagine being anywhere else right now.
- There is a bit of luck to who gets admitted into programs. Many people are highly qualified but spots are limited. In my class there are some people who did not get offers to other programs who seem more qualified than people in my class who did get offers to those programs. However, because spots are limited, realize you really need to do all you can to boost your resume. A high GPA alone won't do it. So if you are rejected and this is really what you want to do with your life, consider what you can do in a year to get more experience in your intended field. Older candidates often have an advantage for this reason—it is difficult to get a lot of experience while still in college.
- I don't recommend entering a master's program if you really want a doctorate. This does not seem to help any more than experience and it will set you back further in reaching your goal.

Chapter 11

TRANSITION TO GRADUATE SCHOOL

So, you're in—you've been accepted to graduate school in psychology. Now what? The application process was arduous, but graduate study itself will require much more motivation, patience, endurance, and work. What have you gotten yourself into? In this chapter we'll take a close look at what graduate school is all about: how it's different from college, characteristics of successful students, and concrete tips for getting organized, managing your newly complicated life, and succeeding in graduate school.

GRADUATE SCHOOL: A NEW BEGINNING

The transition to graduate school means it's time to start honing your memorization skills, and prepping for those late-night cram sessions, right? After all, graduate school is more school, isn't it? Wrong. At the doctoral level, graduate school is a whole different beast—nothing like your undergraduate years. If you enroll in a master's program, you might find that your classes are similar to your undergraduate classes, but if you've enrolled in a doctoral program, get ready for culture shock because there's a qualitative change from undergrad to graduate school. So how is graduate school different from college?

Scope

Undergraduate classes are notorious for cramming vast amounts of information into small chunks of time. As a college student you learned general information on a variety of subjects quickly, without taking the time to get to know any one subject too deeply. Graduate school emphasizes depth. Learning entails developing your expertise in your chosen field—your job is to become an expert.

Expect to encounter more complex assignments and classroom discussions. In graduate school, the emphasis shifts from memorizing information to truly understanding and owning it. You'll now turn to primary sources for your reading and rarely to textbooks. Your classes will emphasize papers and you'll have fewer tests. Moreover, the nature of the tests will change. Nearly all will be essay and perhaps some take-home. Writing and research will be part of every course and the process of inquiry will take precedence. It will no longer be important to remember a fact as much as it is to know how to find it, evaluate it, and use it within your work. You'll come to see knowledge differently—less as a set of facts and more as a construction of evidence and arguments.

New Tasks

You'll no longer write book reports and five to seven page papers on general topics. As a graduate student, your goal in writing class papers is not to show the professor that you've been paying attention, but to demonstrate that you're using the lectures and your reading to synthesize that knowledge into something original and new. You'll discover a great deal of freedom in your choice of topics at this level of academics. You'll have the opportunity to choose paper and research topics that interest you and to approach your work from an angle or perspective that you find useful to your own educational goals. The end to which you strive when working on your papers is not to dazzle your professors with information, but to identify clear, well-supported arguments and to be able to synthesize information, think critically about it, and use it to craft your argument.

During grad school, your job is to learn how to conduct independent and original research and become a specialist within your field. As you move from a generalist to a specialist, your research interests will become more narrow. For example, your research interests will narrow from developmental psychology, for example, to the development of attachment in toddlers. This process of specialization takes time, so read widely and make note of your ideas about what you've read so that you can get a better idea of your interests and become more focused.

Endless Reading

You are likely to panic when you receive the syllabi for your classes and see the long list of suggested or recommended reading. Don't hyperventilate. Very often, professors will create extensive lists of suggested readings—of up to one hundred books. You're not really expected to read them all. Supplemental lists are meant to provide additional references that a student can consult in order to further their understanding of a subject or of the professor's objectives. The list of recommended readings can help you to get the inside perspective on a topic, but rarely are students expected to read and digest them all. Even so, you will find that the assigned readings, those that you are expected to complete, are great—get used to it. Hone your reading skills and devise a system for getting through it all (see the resources in the appendix at the end of this book).

De-Emphasis on Grades

Grades are not the central focus in graduate school. In fact, in graduate school you'll witness tremendous grade inflation. C's are like F's in graduate school; most students get B's or even A's. Only truly inferior work earns C's. Why the grade inflation? Most programs require students who are funded to have a GPA of at least 3.0 or 3.3; therefore professors assign few poor grades. This doesn't mean that you can slack off, though, because the courses will be quite demanding. In addition, you'll want to perform well to enhance and maintain your reputation among professors and attract invitations to conduct research (and get funding).

Emphasis on Professional Development

You are embarking on a process of professional socialization. You will learn how to become a professional in your field by observing the work of your mentor, and also by observing more advanced graduate students. This emphasis on professional development goes way beyond what you've experienced as an undergraduate student. You'll learn more than academic skills, but professional skills, like how to maintain a productive laboratory, how to give a research talk, how to teach, and how to be a psychologist. You'll attend academic conferences in your discipline, where professors and graduate students present their research and network. You'll get an inside glimpse at how professors think and learn about how to publish papers in scholarly journals. Throughout all of this, your goal is to learn how to become a professional, establish your own academic niche—your specialty—and get known for it.

Generating Knowledge

Graduate study entails a fundamental leap from being an acquirer of knowledge to a generator of knowledge. As you take courses, begin to consider your research interests. What are the important, unanswered questions in your field? How does your own research relate to those questions? What other people have tried to answer research questions similar to your own? What other techniques can be used to address your own research questions? You will not be able to answer all these questions through your coursework. Instead, you'll do your own outside reading to explore these questions and develop your research agenda.

Relationships Matter

Networking is the key to success in graduate school and beyond. Get to know other students and professors because your contacts will help you further your research, become known, and get a job after graduation. Professional contacts can lead to guest speaking opportunities, invitations to join conference presentation panels, research leads, letters of recommendations, and introductions to powerful professionals in your field. Many new graduate students are surprised to learn that their reputation does not rest on their academic credentials alone—relationships matter. As a graduate student, you'll develop closer relationships with faculty but will also be more dependent on them for your success. Under the best circumstances, you will develop a nurturing and mentoring relationship with a faculty member. Later in this chapter we'll talk about mentors and how they can further your professional development

Establish Independence

While your relationship with your mentor or advisor is critical to your existence in graduate school, you must also develop independence. You must learn to work without direct supervision–to take initiative and survive and thrive on your own. It will be up to you to get your coursework done, make time for your advisor's research, get your own research done, and take charge of your classroom (if you have a teaching assignment). It's your responsibility to find out the requirements and ensure that you're meeting them. Actively educate yourself about what lies ahead. Take initiative and learn everything about the program up front. Ask questions before something goes wrong.

In graduate school you'll develop your own identity. The next few years will represent a transformation from student to another social identity–psychologist. In some ways, you're becoming a new person and the transition will be challenging. Sometimes it may be difficult to know exactly what it is you should be learning. You may find it hard to differentiate yourself from your advisor. A helpful way to help you make the identity transformation is to talk with other researchers. As a college student you might have only talked with a professor or TA when you had a problem or question. In graduate school you should talk with other students, post-docs, and faculty about your research as often as possible to practice explaining it, get feedback, and to get new ideas.

Politics

Many students are surprised by the political side of graduate school. You'll get to see the behind the scenes activity as you didn't as an undergraduate student and see that politics influences departmental life. Not all professors get along and there are sometimes struggles and arguments for power. What do I mean by politics? Politics is about who is allowed to do what and who gets the resources (money, people, equipment, etc.). Anytime there are limited resources, people scramble for them and arguments can break out among faculty. Successful students are aware of political tensions and understand them and have the social skills to maneuver to accomplish what they need without losing their interest in the subject. Avoid sticky situations and disagreements among faculty. Don't gossip–it will come back to bite you!

Clearly, graduate school is very different from college. The biggest difference is that graduate school is a job. You are a professional student. The contacts that you make during graduate school will be essential to your later career. You will attend conferences, give papers, and publish your research in an attempt to become known by the academic community. How can you get used to this new situation? First, attend any and all orientation sessions that your department and university offers. Second, understand that it's normal to experience mixed emotions. You're probably excited to start your professional career, but also anxious because you're starting something new. You might feel particularly uneasy because though you stood out as an undergraduate, your graduate school peers were also at the top of their classes. Third, follow the advice that appears throughout the remainder of this chapter on how to ease your transition to graduate school.

CHARACTERISTICS OF SUCCESSFUL STUDENTS

What does it take to succeed in graduate school? Graduate school faculty name the following characteristics as essential for excelling in graduate school (Appleby, 1990):

- *Visibility.* You must make yourself known and be visible in your department to make contacts, develop networks, and get ahead in your research. Successful students are visible in the sense that they spend time in their department–often after working hours.
- *Hardworking.* Of course a graduate degree is hard work. Faculty tend to perceive students who excel as hard workers. The key to gaining a positive reputation among faculty is to be seen working in visible places, like your office or the department, rather than at home.
- *Interest in Research.* Many students in applied programs, like clinical and counseling psychology programs, assume that practice-related skills take precedence over research. Students who plan to be clinicians also must work at developing their research skills because

good clinicians can grasp and conduct solid research. Students who excel get involved in research beyond their theses and research assistantships. They view research as an essential part of psychology, are intellectually curious, and spend time conducting and writing up research in addition to their required projects (e.g., theses).

- *Mentor.* The most successful graduate students develop mentoring relationships with one or more faculty—close relationships that allow students to learn and grow into colleagues. Students who excel are perceived well by faculty. They're seen as easy to teach and good at accepting feedback.

As you can see, what makes graduate students successful is something other than just intelligence—it's a combination of motivation, commitment, and maturity. As you enter graduate school, get clear on your goals and identify ways to meet them and grow during your graduate student years. There's much to learn and you have a large role in where graduate school takes you. Take initiative, develop a strong work ethic, and connect with faculty to excel in graduate school and develop professional skills to last a lifetime.

YOUR RELATIONSHIP WITH YOUR ADVISOR AND MENTOR

Faculty play an enormous role in your graduate education. Not just during class, but outside of class too. Your relationship with your advisor is essential to successfully completing your graduate program and your dissertation. What should you look for in an advisor? How do you navigate the murky waters of student-advisor relationships? Where can you find a mentor? How do you develop mentoring skills?

Differences Between Advisors and Mentors

Many students use the terms "advisor" and "mentor" interchangeably. An *advisor* is often assigned to you by the graduate program. Your advisor helps you select courses and often directs your thesis or dissertation. Your advisor may or may not become your mentor. A *mentor* is much more than an advisor. A mentoring relationship is a close relationship that develops over time between a student and faculty member and is characterized by guidance and caring. A mentor guides you towards growth and development—he or she becomes a trusted ally and guides you through the graduate and postdoctoral years. In science, mentoring often takes the form of an apprenticeship relationship. The mentor aids the student in scientific instruction, but perhaps more importantly, socializes the student to the norms of the scientific community. Your mentor will help you to learn and internalize the values, norms, and practices of the discipline. Mentors provide support in addition to training.

Mentoring is important because graduate school is different in that your goal is to contribute to knowledge rather than merely attain it as you did as an undergraduate student. Mentor relationships can help you to learn the skills needed for success—more than book knowledge but professional norms and values. It's a process of socialization. Students who have mentoring relationships have a higher level of productivity, are more involved with their departments, and are more satisfied.

Choosing a Mentor

Ideally your advisor will become your mentor, but that is not always the case. How do you choose a mentor? What characteristics should you look for?

A mentor should:

- provide you with support and encouragement
- help you to learn from your mistakes
- offer opportunities for collaboration, joint presentations, and departmental talks
- help you to learn about writing and submitting manuscripts for publication
- be interested in your career area
- be able to provide support and training in your area
- model a successful academic career and training in your area
- be committed to help mentees make the next move in their career development
- demonstrate personal integrity
- introduce you to colleagues
- help you to identify and work with your strengths and weaknesses
- provide opportunities for you to develop independence

Take Your Advisor's Perspective

Not all students get to develop a mentoring relationship. Some have merely advisors–faculty who provide advice but don't truly guide them in an apprenticeship. Other students have both relationships, but with different faculty members–a mentor and an advisor. How do you manage your advisor? Take off your "student" hat and imagine the world from your advisor's perspective. It's unfortunate, but for many faculty, advising doesn't fall high on the list of priorities. It's not that they're evil; they're just being practical. Most academic institutions provide little to no recognition for advising students. Advising doesn't count towards salary increases, promotion, or prestige. Because of this, many faculty place their advising duties on the back burner, after tasks that are more critical to tenure and promotion (i.e., research). Yes, most faculty are interested in working with others on ground-breaking research, however few dissertations are of that magnitude. It's not fair, but unfortunately, it is often (though not always) the truth.

Have Reasonable Expectations

If you want to survive grad school and the dissertation process, you'll need to develop reasonable expectations of your advisor's role. It is difficult to develop realistic expectations because there are few recognized advising standards with which to measure your experience. Most institutions set a general code of ethics and establish a quota on how many students an advisor can take on. Other than that, there are few guidelines. Some universities set general role descriptions, such as meet with students, read and return drafts in a reasonable amount of time, and monitor progress, but don't set more specific requirements. In addition, professors are not taught how to advise but learn on the fly, often using their own experiences as a guide. In some cases, advisors are just as clueless as students.

Protect Your Interests

Given this lousy state of advising affairs, graduate students must take an active role in planning their studies. Protect your career by gathering as much information as you can; be your own advisor. What does this mean? Take responsibility for discovering your degree require-ments and for determining what experience you'll need to succeed in your chosen career. A variety of web and print resources exist for stu-dents who wish to succeed in grad school (see the appendix). Take advantage of these resources and use them wisely.

Although you take an active role in charting your graduate education and career, your advisor is still a crucial element of grad school success that you can't ignore. Your advisor can pull strings, write letters on your behalf, and help you in finding a job or postdoctoral position after graduation. Don't sever ties with your advisor! Instead, remember that you have the primary responsibility for maintaining the student-advisor relationship. Frequently update your advisor on your progress, seek advice, and be active in fostering the relationship. Understand that your advisor is busy and probably advises other students as well. As a scientist and professional, you must learn to think independently. Your advisor's role is to help you to make that transition, but you've got to help him or her out.

Understand the Other Side: Learn About Mentoring

Perhaps one way to gain insight into the mentoring relationship is to learn a little bit about the other side: how to mentor. There are many benefits of mentoring for faculty (University of Michigan, 2002):

- Access to new collaborators
- Research assistants
- Increasing professional stature by shaping future scholars
- Keeping abreast of new knowledge by being exposed to students with many questions and who are learning about cutting edge research
- Personal satisfaction in aiding a student's development

What do faculty look for in mentees (University of Michigan, 2002)?

- *Mutual Interests.* How do your interests intersect with theirs? How do your prior experiences relate to the faculty member's research?
- *Motivation and Direction.* Faculty look for students who are eager to grow and move on to the next state of their professional develop-ment. Share your goals and ask for their advice on how you can

work towards these goals. Does he or she suggest any specific courses to take or projects to get involved with?

- *Initiative.* Establishing the relationship is your task. Interact with professors outside of class. Ask questions about the material and demonstrate your interest and ability to take initiative.
- *Skills and Strengths.* What do you bring to the table? Faculty look for students who have skills to assist them in furthering their research. Be ready to explain to faculty why they should invest in you.

What do faculty need to know about being good mentors and how can this knowledge help you establish a mentoring relationship? Throughout your graduate school years, you'll spend countless hours honing your research and methodological skills, learning how to think critically, and becoming socialized into your professional role. Will you really be prepared for a faculty position, though? Most new faculty lament that they are unprepared for a critical aspect of their job: mentoring and supervising students. These tips for mentors might help you to gain insight into your mentor's perspective and help in doing his or her job.

Make Personal Contact

Engage students in an ongoing conversation and relationship. Say "hello" in the hall and take a moment to ask, "How's it going?" Be available and let students know that they're welcome to visit during your office hours. Make contact at least once each semester. If a student becomes distant or is in danger of falling through the cracks, a simple phone call can help to engage them.

What this means for you, the graduate student: Make contact with your mentor—make it easy for him or her to establish an advising relationship.

Take the Mystery out of Grad School

Be familiar with your departmental and university guidelines and remember that new students often are unaware of policies, procedures, and even what questions to ask. Clarify the requirements for coursework, practica, comprehensive exams, research, and teaching.

What this means for you, the graduate student: Ask questions about depart-mental and university requirements. Read all that you can about depart-mental requirements for course work and so on—and ask your advisor to confirm what you've learned and clarify questions.

Provide Feedback

Provide timely, constructive, and supportive assessments of student work. Provide praise, when it is deserved. When students fall behind, engage them in a conversation rather than assume a lack of commit-ment. Falling behind can signal personal problems, depression, social isolation, and exhaustion. Address potential problems early. Putting problems aside, hoping that they will improve on their own over time, may be more damaging to students.

What this means for you, the graduate student: Provide your advisor with samples of your work. Let your advisor know when you're experiencing prob-lems that affect your work.

Provide Encouragement and Support

Many graduate students suffer from "imposter syndrome." Students often are anxious, insecure, and wonder whether they really belong in a graduate program. Explain that most grad students feel like imposters at one time or another. Share your experience and provide support. Help students by teaching them to break large tasks (like the disserta-tion) into smaller ones to avoid feeling overwhelmed. Encourage stu-dents to talk to you and be approachable.

What this means for you, the graduate student: Touch base with your advisor frequently—at least once or twice a semester. Ask your advisor questions that will elicit advice and support (e.g., "Were you ever anxious when you were a graduate student?"). Sometimes advisors are more than willing to provide support but need a little nudge or reminder.

Support Professional Development

Provide opportunities for students to demonstrate and enhance their competence. Invite students to important meetings and professional conferences so that they can gain insight into the academic environment and gain visibility. Encourage students to make presentations at conferences and to apply for fellowships. Promote your student's work.

What this means for you, the graduate student: Look for opportunities to promote your professional development and bring them to the attention of your advisor. Summer fellowships, conference announcements, and requests for proposals or papers are great learning opportunities. Bring them to the attention of your advisor and ask for feedback about whether you should apply—or for help applying.

Graduate Student Responsibilities

You play a large role in whether you get the mentoring that you need. How can you make it more likely that you'll fulfill your mentoring needs?

- Keep in touch with your mentor. Keep your mentor informed about your progress. Notify your mentor when problems arise and seek his or her input and advice.
- Become a colleague. Remember that your mentor has something to gain in this relationship too. Contribute knowledge, when you can. You're learning many new things and may read articles that can help your mentor's research. Let him or her know when you encounter research that is of interest. Your mentor will welcome your contributions as evidence of his or her skill as mentor.
- Seek advice from others. No one person can fulfill all of your mentoring needs. Seek advice from whoever is best prepared to meet your needs. You might go to one person for advice about research, another about teaching, and a third about job searching. Don't expect to get it all from one person. Advanced students and postdocs are great sources of information—all of your mentors don't have to be faculty. Also understand that mentoring relationships change over time. Most of us have several mentors over the course of our careers: mentors for different areas (e.g., teaching and research) and at different times in our professional development (e.g., grad student, post-doc, junior faculty).
- Respect faculty time (University of Michigan, 2002). Show up for meetings on time. Accept responsibility for running meetings in the sense that you should be prepared to raise issues and concerns and allow the professor's role to be to respond and advise. After-

wards, summarize agreements that have been reached and email the summary, an explanation of what you have agreed to do for your next meeting, and a request for a response if your message contains inaccuracies or errors. If your mentor is facing a work-related emergency (e.g., a deadline), offer to reschedule. Part of respecting faculty time is waiting to submit papers for their feedback until the papers are in a high-quality form (don't submit rough drafts unless he or she requests them). Also, don't ask a professor to reread an entire paper if you've only revised certain sections; point out the revisions.

- Clarify expectations. What does the faculty member consider to be a normal workload? How many hours should you be spending on your research per week? How often does he or she expect to meet? How often will he or she provide feedback?
- Learn how to respond to criticism appropriately. Accept critiques in a professional manner. Listen to the points and take time to consider them before responding.
- Follow your mentor's advice. Read the books and articles that they suggest and let them know what you think so that they see that their time and mentoring is being put to good use.
- Respect boundaries. Friendships often develop between mentor and protégé. Even so, remember that the relationship is still of a hierarchical nature–they are still in a supervisory position over you. Take that into consideration before revealing personal information. Also be careful about overstaying your welcome and taking too much time from your mentor during each visit.
- Come to meetings prepared. Have a list of topics to discuss, plan for what you hope to get out of the meeting, summary of what you have done since your last meeting, list of any upcoming deadlines, and notes from prior meetings.

EASING YOUR TRANSITION

It's easy to feel overwhelmed during those first few months of graduate school. Who am I kidding? It's easy to feel overwhelmed throughout much of grad school! The best advice for avoiding burnout and getting bogged down is to keep track of your days, maintain daily progress towards your goals, and work towards easing your transition to graduate school so that you can build healthy habits that will last throughout your scholarly career.

Getting Organized: How Do You Begin?

Graduate education provides students with the opportunity to develop and hone a host of essential scholarly skills. However, students receive little training in the most important skill of all, the skill that will make or break their professional careers: organization. Lose the clutter and get a handle on your academic career by getting organized.

Now you're probably wondering, "how will organization make or break my career?" Think about it. Being unorganized is a time waster. The unorganized student spends precious time searching for papers, files, notes, wondering which pile to check first. She forgets and misses meetings or arrives late, repeatedly. He finds it hard to focus on the task at hand because his mind is swimming with the details of what must be done next or what should have been done yesterday. Face it. A disorganized office is a sign of a cluttered mind. Cluttered minds are inefficient for scholarly productivity. So how do you get organized? Try these tips:

Use a Calendar System

By now, you probably use a calendar to keep track of weekly appointments and meetings. Grad school requires taking a long-term perspective on time. Use a yearly, monthly, and weekly calendar.

- *Year Scale.* It's difficult to keep track of today *and* remember what needs to be done in 6 months. Long-term deadlines for financial aid, conference submissions, and grant proposals creep up quickly. Plan at least two years ahead with a yearly calendar, divided into months. Add all long-term deadlines on this calendar. When do you register for classes? Your calendar is also useful for keeping track of where you've been. For example, when did you submit that journal article? Is it time to follow up?
- *Month Scale.* Your monthly calendar will include all paper deadlines, test dates, assignments, and appointments. Your goal is to put your month on paper so that you can plan ahead and ensure

that you make the time to get it all done. Break large assignments and tasks into their component parts and add self-imposed deadlines. For example, break a term paper into many smaller and more manageable tasks such as finding a topic, conducting literature searches, gathering articles and books, reading and taking notes, writing an outline, writing the first draft, and revising. Your self-imposed deadlines will help you to keep on task and get the work done on time. Many students use a large wall-mounted monthly calendar so that they can see everything at a glance and it's always in the same place.

- *Week Scale.* Use a weekly academic planner and carry it everywhere. Here is where you organize your daily life. Include all of your day-to-day appointments and deadlines (imposed by others as well as yourself). Have a study group on Thursday afternoon? Record it here. When are you planning to do the library research for your next paper? Block out time in your weekly planner.

Use a To-Do List

Each day create a to-do list (more on that below) and a rough schedule for getting everything done. Use a to-do list to free your mind for the work at hand and keep you moving towards your goals on a daily basis. Take ten minutes every night and make a to-do list for the next day. Look over your calendar for the next couple of weeks to remember tasks that need to be planned in advance: searching for literature for that term paper, buying and sending birthday cards, and preparing submissions to conferences and grants. Your to-do list is your friend; never leave home without it. Write in all your assignments, chores (like laundry!), and other tasks (e.g., holiday shopping). Prioritize the items so you don't waste time on nonessential tasks. When is that paper due? Is it high priority? Place all high-priority tasks first. Regularly stop and ask yourself, "What is the best use of my time right now? What needs to get done now?" Do that task. Prioritize your to-do list.

Keep a Daily Schedule

Set up a flexible daily schedule that helps you determine what to do with each hour of your day. With all the tasks you'll juggle as a graduate student, you can't afford to lose a day or even a few hours.

- Regardless of how busy you are, schedule time to work on classes and research *every* day, even if it is just a few 20-minute blocks. Think you can't get much done in 20 minutes? You'd be surprised. What's more important is that the material will stay fresh in your mind, enabling you to reflect on it at unexpected times (like on your ride to school or walk to the library).
- Be flexible. Allow time for interruptions and distractions. Plan about 50 to 60 percent of your time so that you'll have the flexibility to handle unexpected interruptions. When you're interrupted, ask yourself, "What is the most important thing I can do right now? What's most urgent?" Use your answer to plan your time and get back on track.
- Schedule time for breaks. You can't study for an exam or write a paper if you're fried. Take a 15- to 20-minute break every once in a while to stretch your legs, get something to eat, or play a video game. Go for a short walk; the exercise will wake you up and sharpen your thinking. Plus a quiet walk is like meditation. It gives you a chance to work out problems, think, or just "veg-out."
- Go with your flow. Think about your biological peaks and lows. Are you a morning person? Or are you at your best at night? Plan your day accordingly. Save your most difficult work for the times when you're at your best.
- Say "No." Sometimes we take on too much. Whether it's extra courses, job responsibilities, or extracurricular activities, consider how important each is to you before agreeing. This is a hard one, I know! Before agreeing to take on any new responsibilities, sleep on it. Say, "Sounds like a great opportunity. Let me take time to think about it and get back to you tomorrow." Sleep on it and if it still seems like a good idea in the morning—and if it still seems that you have the time and energy for it—then go ahead.
- Plan time to have fun. It's easy to lose yourself in your work. The fact is there will always be work to do—something that you could be doing with your time. Make taking time for yourself a priority because otherwise you might find your graduate school years fly by with many professional accomplishments, but no life. Just as you schedule time for work, schedule time for fun. You'll be healthier and more productive when you have downtime.

Make Use of Wasted Time

Another way to take control is to get more done by using your time more effectively. Carry pocket work, something that you can do while waiting. Whether it's reading for the train, or flash cards to study. Ten minutes here, fifteen there; it adds up. Plus, cognitive psychology research on memory has shown that we can recall more information if we work and study in short periods rather than long ones, so you just might learn more.

Organize Your Study Space

Choose a quiet place that is well lit. Hang your monthly calendar on the wall to help you keep on track. Strip your study space of all distracting items and make it a pleasant and motivating place to work. Keep your desk away from the television or anything else that might distract you. Think of it as a form of cocooning–intellectual cocooning whereby you create a motivating, healthy, and nurturing place to work. Essentially you're creating your own world, a place to work–a barrier between you and the world.

Make sure that your desk is large enough. While in grad school, I used a conference table so that I had space for my computer and to spread out various books and articles at once. Choose a sturdy, comfortable chair. Remember that you'll spend a great deal of time in this chair, so choose wisely and invest in a pillow to support your lower back and reduce back pain. Finally, keep all of your supplies handy to minimize time spent searching for items and minimize potential distractions. Organize your space to maximize your efficiency, keeping supplies near your work space.

Splurge on Office Supplies

Though office supplies can be expensive, it's easier to get organized when you've got the right tools. Purchase a quality stapler, paper clips, binder clips in various sizes, small and large stick-on notes, sticky flags for marking important pages in text, and plenty of paper. Buy a filing cabinet or file crates and boxes of file folders, hanging folders, and labels. Go to a supply store and purchase office supplies in bulk to save money and ensure that you don't run out of supplies unexpectedly. Having the right tools makes keeping organized easy.

Set Up a Filing System

In your filing cabinet or set of file crates, organize your filing system. Don't skimp on file folders or you'll find yourself doubling up on files and lose track of your most important papers. Maintain files for research/thesis ideas, thesis references (probably divided up into additional files for each topic), exam material (as you prepare for comprehensive exams you'll probably store copies of old exams and study materials), professional credentials (vita, sample cover letter, research statement, etc.), reprints and professional articles (organized by topic), life (bills, taxes, etc.), teaching materials (organized by topic).

Start a Research Journal

Getting down and dirty with research is critical to your success in graduate school, you know that. But just how do you get started? Where do great research ideas come from? How do you figure out what to research? Great research ideas can come out of nowhere–but don't count on yours to just pop on like a light bulb.

Look for ideas systematically and at all times. Does that mean that you must constantly rack your brain looking for a topic? No! Just keep your mind open to new ideas and capture them quickly for more in-depth consideration later. Keep a journal of your ideas and activities as an ongoing log of your thoughts about your research.

What do you write in your research journal?

- Interesting questions
- Problems
- Possible solutions
- References to read
- Notes on articles and papers you've read

Begin your journal early in your graduate school career–long before you're searching for a dissertation topic. Don't plan to share your journal with anyone–write freely.

When you read an interesting article, note it in your journal:

- What was the research topic?
- How did they study it?
- What did they find?
- What ideas did the authors suggest for further research?
- What was striking about the article?
- What are your own ideas?

Every now and then, read your journal. Over time you may notice themes, thoughts that seem to connect, and patterns. Recurring themes will suggest avenues for research to form your dissertation. Sure, not everything that you capture in your journal will fit into your future research, but a journal is an important way of learning about your research interests, defining them, and crafting workable ideas.

As you find potential dissertation ideas, thoroughly read the related literature, noting your thoughts in your journal. You'll never complete your review of the literature as new articles are constantly being published. Don't wait to finish your literature review to start your research or you will be forever reading and never conducting research. Be aware of the literature in your area and note how your work is different from others.

When you begin your research, note its progress in your journal. Write down questions, problems that emerge, and notes on your methodology and results. Your research journal is a record of what you hypothesized, did, and found, as well as a place to consider the implications of your work. Continue to read current articles about your topic and record your comments in your journal. You'll find your journal, your research record, invaluable as you write your dissertation.

Deal with Stress

Graduate students often find themselves suffering from a mixture of stress, exhaustion, and low motivation. Lots of graduate students are susceptible to feeling stressed out and blue. Don't let a lack of motivation hurt your performance and success in graduate school. What can you do about low motivation and stress? Take care of yourself!

Recognize the Signs of Stress

You know when you're stressed, right? Just remember that the signs are more pervasive than you think! Usually when we think of stress symptoms, we think of high blood pressure, elevated heart rate, overeating, and sweating too much. Signs of stress also include irritability, insomnia, anxiety, headaches, indigestion, muscle tension, and jitteriness.

Learn How to Relax

Easier said than done, you say? Take the time to learn relaxation techniques, as they'll help you all throughout grad school and the rest of your life. For example, practice the relaxation response, a form of meditation.

Find a quiet environment (a room at home, school, the library) where you can be alone without distractions. Get into a comfortable position, preferably with your spine straight. Try sitting down cross-legged or in the lotus position. Don't lie down or you might fall asleep! During the relaxation session, focus your concentration on an object, word, or phrase. This is your point of focus. Begin to breathe deeply and slowly. Inhale through your nose. As you exhale through your mouth, repeat your chosen word or phrase. Concentrate on your point of focus and don't worry about your thought processes. It is difficult to eliminate distracting thoughts, but instead concentrate on your point of focus. Try not to dwell on your distracting thoughts; let them slip away. Continue for 10 to 20 minutes and you'll feel more relaxed and at peace.

Try a Soothing Bath

Close the bathroom door and run a warm bubble bath. Add a few drops of an essential oil like lavender for an extra fragrant bath. Light a few candles, turn down the lights, and soak. Don't think about what needs to be done; just experience the warm water and simply be. As you soak, try some deep breathing exercises and meditate to move towards experiencing inner peace.

Be Realistic

When you begin to feel tense and overwhelmed, stop what you're doing and try to look at your situation from a fresh perspective. Ask yourself, "Why am I feeling this way? If this task doesn't get done, what's the worst thing that can happen? What is the absolute minimum that I need to do to complete this task?" Be realistic. Every assignment does not have to be perfect. If your assignment isn't perfect, is it really the end of the world? A year from now, will it be important? All too often we get stressed out over everyday things whose consequences are minimal. Try to look at the "big picture."

Don't Cut Corners on Your Health

It's all too easy to skip a workout or pull an all-nighter to finish your work, but it's more important than ever to take care of yourself when you're under stress. When you're feeling stressed, the immune system functions less effectively and you're more likely to get sick. You know how far behind you fall when you get sick! It's difficult, but essential that you maintain a healthy diet, get regular exercise, and plenty of sleep to function your best and get rid of the grad student blues.

Seek Social Support

Seek out faculty and graduate students for help in addressing any of your concerns. Look to others for social support. Advanced students are usually willing to help you if you just ask them. Also, although your new peers may not be expressing their uncertainties and so not appear to be stressed, just know that they are. Try opening up to them, and you will soon see that you are all in the same boat.

Exhibit 14. Tips from Graduate Students

- Try to find a graduate advisor who matches your research or clinical interests as well as your working style and work habits or you may find yourself miserable.
- Try to get whatever you can from your classes. Use class papers as opportunities to review the literature in your area of interests and gather information that will be useful for your own research and dissertation while fulfilling the course requirements.
- Be prepared to do a lot of reading!
- Never doubt yourself. If you got into grad school, you have the talent to succeed. Believe in yourself.

- Work hard. You have rights. Don't let yourself be bullied by faculty members. It's intimidating, but don't let yourself be a puppet for your department.
- Talk with other graduate students. Seek their advice.
- Remember that if you're struggling, someone else is too. You're only human—ask for help when you need it.
- Set up a schedule and plan out your time.
- Try not to take it too seriously.
- The first year is the hardest year. Graduate school success is not a race, but a marathon. Keep in there.
- Don't make enemies. If you're having a difficult relationship with someone, find a way to improve it.
- Rely on your classmates and eliminate competitiveness. Build a support network in and outside of your program.
- Don't take feedback or criticism personally. It's part of the training, but left out of the brochure. Develop a thick skin so that you can continue to do the work and maintain perspective.
- Be careful in picking your advisor. Don't be afraid to change advisors if you can't get along or the relationship isn't working. The advisor relationship is too important to mess up, so take care.
- Expect ambiguity and a lack of clear direction.
- Learn quickly to prioritize. You simply will not be able to do everything that is asked of you. Become invested in your work but understand that everything may not get done. You also need to claim time for yourself to do things you love, find relaxing, etc.
- Build a support system within your program. No matter how supportive other friends and family members may be, they simply will not understand what you are going through and the stresses you encounter. Having a support system of people who can truly relate to your experience and who can also offer practical help, like studying together, is invaluable.
- You're in school to learn. Consider the practical application of the material you are learning to make it meaningful for you. Having the knowledge about a subject to survive a test is no longer the goal—you will need to utilize this knowledge in the field. Especially if you're a clinician, your knowledge not only will impact your success as a practitioner, but also the lives of those who you treat. You should feel responsible for acquiring the appropriate knowledge base to make yourself a competent and ethical psychologist.

APPENDIX

RECOMMENDED READING

Career Exploration

Andrews, L. L. (1997). *How to Choose a College Major.* Chicago, IL: NTC Publishing Group.

Brown, D. (Editor) (2002). *Career Choice and Development* (4th Edition). San Francisco: Jossey-Bass.

Buckingham, M., & Clifton, D. O. (2001). *Now, Discover Your Strengths.* New York: Free Press.

Johnston, S. M. (1998). *The Career Adventure: Your Guide to Personal Assessment, Career Exploration, and Decision-Making.* Upper Saddle River, NJ: Prentice Hall.

Reeves, D. L., & Bradbury, M. J. (1998). *Majors Exploration: A Search and Find Guide for College and Career Direction.* Upper Saddle River, NJ: Prentice Hall.

Careers in Psychology

Keller, P. A. (1994). *Academic Paths: Career Decisions and Experiences of Psychologists.* Hillsdale, NJ: Erlbaum.

Kuther, T. L. (2004). *Your Career in Psychology: Clinical and Counseling Psychology.* Pacific Grove: Wadsworth.

Kuther, T. L. (2004). *Your Career in Psychology: Industrial/Organizational and Human Factors Psychology.* Pacific Grove, CA: Wadsworth.

Kuther, T. L. (2004). *Your Career in Psychology: Psychology and Law.* Pacific Grove, CA: Wadsworth.

Kuther, T. L. & Morgan, R. D. (2004). *Careers in Psychology: Opportunities in a Changing World.* Pacific Grove, CA: Wadsworth.

Sternberg, R. J. (1997). *Career Paths in Psychology: Where Your Degree Can Take You.* Washington, DC: American Psychological Association.

Woody, R. H., & Robertson, M. H. (1997). *A Career in Clinical Psychology: From Training to Employment.* Madison, CT: International Universities Press.

Graduate School Admissions

American Psychological Association. (1997). *Getting In: A Step-by-Step Plan for Gaining Admission to Graduate School in Psychology.* Washington, DC: Author.

Jerrard, R., & Jerrard, M. (1998). *The Grad School Handbook: An Insider's Guide to Getting in and Succeeding.* New York: Perigee.

Kaplan (1997). *Getting into Grad School: Selection, Admissions, Financial Aid* (Serial). New York: Simon & Schuster.

Keith-Spiegel, P., & Wiederman, M. W. (2000). *The Complete Guide to Graduate School Admission: Psychology, Counseling, and Related Professions.* Mahwah, NJ: Erlbaum.

Mumby, D. G. (1997). *Graduate School: Winning Strategies for Getting in With or Without Excellent Grades.* Quebec, Canada: Proto Press.

Locating Graduate Programs

American Psychological Association. (2003). *Graduate Study in Psychology,* 36th Edition. Washington, DC: Author.

Buskist, W., & Mixon, A. (1997). *Allyn & Bacon Guide to Master's Programs in Psychology.* Needham Heights, MA: Allyn & Bacon.

Norcross, J. C., Sayette, M. A., & Mayne, T. J. (2002). *Insider's Guide to Graduate Programs in Clinical and Counseling Psychology: 2002/2003 Edition.* New York: Guilford Press.

Petersons. (2003). *Petersons Graduate Programs in Psychology 2004 (Peterson's Decision Guides: Graduate Programs).* Lawrenceville, NJ: Petersons Guides.

Financial Aid: Paying for Graduate School

Blum, L. (2000). *Free Money for Graduate School.* New York: Checkmark Books.

Cassidy, D., & Cassidy, D. J. (2000). *Dan Cassidy's Worldwide Graduate Scholarship Directory: Thousands of Top Scholarships Throughout the United States and Around the World.* Franklin Lakes, NJ: Career Press.

Hamel, A. V., Heiberger, M. M., & Vick, J. M. (2002). *The Graduate School Funding Handbook, 2nd Edition.* Philadelphia: University of Pennsylvania Press.

McKee, P. C., & McKee, C. R. (2003). *Cash for Grad School: The Ultimate Guide to Grad School Scholarships.* New York: Quill.

Petersons. (1998). *Peterson's Grants for Graduate & Post Doctoral Study.* Lawrenceville, NJ: Petersons Guides.

Petersons. (2002). *Petersons Getting Money for Graduate School.* Lawrenceville, NJ: Petersons Guides.

The Graduate Record Exam

Bobrow, J. (1985). *Math Review for Standardized Tests.* Hoboken, NJ: Cliff Notes.

Easy-Prep Flash Cards. (1997). *GRE Vocabulary Set 1: With 750 Flash Cards and Study Guide.* Easy-Prep.

Green, S. W., Wolf, I. K., & Green, S. W. (2002). *Barron's How to Prepare for the GRE Graduate Record Examination* Hauppauge, NY: Barrons Educational Series.

Jay, M. (2002). *Cracking the GRE Psychology Test*. Lawrenceville, NJ: Princeton Review.

Kaplan. (2002). *Kaplan GRE Verbal Workbook, 2nd Edition*. New York: Kaplan.

Kellogg, R. T. (2000). *Best Preparation for the GRE Psychology*. Piscataway, NJ: Research & Education Assn.

Lighthouse Review Inc. (1999). *The Ultimate Math Refresher for the GRE, GMAT, and SAT*. Austin, TX.

Lighthouse Review Inc. (2001). *The Ultimate Verbal and Vocabulary Builder for the SAT, ACT, GRE, GMAT and LSAT*. Austin, TX.

Lurie, K. (2002). *Cracking the GRE 2003: With Four Complete Practice Tests on Cd-Rom*. Lawrenceville, NJ: Princeton Review.

Palmer, E. L., & Thompson-Schill, S. L. (2001). *Barron's How to Prepare for The GRE Psychology: Graduate Record Examination in Psychology*. Hauppauge, NY: Barrons Educational Series.

Dealing with Test Anxiety

Casbarro, J. (2003). *Test Anxiety & What You Can Do About It*. Port Chester, NY: National Professional Resources, Inc.

Devine, J., Divine, J., & Klyen, D. W. (1982). *How to Beat Test Anxiety and Score Higher on the SAT and All Other Exams*. Hauppauge, NY: Barrons Educational Series.

Johnson, S. (1997). *Taking the Anxiety Out of Taking Tests: A Step-By-Step Guide*. Oakland, CA: New Harbinger Pubns.

Personal Statements

McKinney, A. (2000). *Real Essays for College and Grad School (Real-Resumes Series)*. Fayetteville, NC: PREP Publishing.

Richardson, J. (2000). *Mastering the Personal Statement*. Toronto, Canada: Richardson Press.

Staw, J. (2003). *Unstuck : A Supportive and Practical Guide to Working Through Writer's Block*. New York: St. Martin's Press.

Stelzer, R. J. (1997). *How to Write a Winning Personal Statement for Graduate and Professional School*. Lawrenceville, NJ: Petersons Guides.

Curriculum Vitae

Anthony, R., & Roe, G. (1998). *The Curriculum Vitae Handbook: How to Present and Promote Your Academic Career*. Iowa City, IA: Rudi Publishing.

Geckeis, K., & Acy, L. (2003). *How to Prepare Your Curriculum Vitae*. New York McGraw-Hill/Contemporary Books.

Jackson, A. L. (1998). *Prepare Your Curriculum Vitae*. New York: McGraw-Hill.

The Interview

Deluca, M. J. (1996). *Best Answers to the 201 Most Frequently Asked Interview Questions.* New York: McGraw-Hill.

Fry, R. W. (2000). *101 Great Answers to the Toughest Interview Questions,* Franklin Lakes, NJ: Career Press.

Kador, J. (2002). *201 Best Questions To Ask On Your Interview.* New York: McGraw-Hill.

Medley, A. H. (1992). *Sweaty Palms: The Neglected Art of Being Interviewed.* Berkeley, CA: Ten Speed Press.

Stein, M. (2001). *Fearless Interviewing: What to Do Before, During and After an Interview.* Lincoln, NE: iUniverse.com.

Transition to Graduate School

Cryer, P. (2000). *The Research Student's Guide to Success.* New York: Open University.

Delamont, S., Atkinson, P., & Parry, O. (1999). *Survival and Success in Graduate School: Disciplines, Disciples and the Doctorate.* New York: Routledge Falmer.

Ellis, D. (2000). *Becoming a Master Student: Tools, Techniques, Hints, Ideals, Illustrations, Examples, Methods, Procedures, Processes, Skills, Resources, and Suggestions for Success.* New York: Houghton Mifflin.

Farmer, V. L. (2003). *The Black Student's Guide to Graduate and Professional School Success.* New York: Praeger Publishers.

Johnson, W. B., & Huwe, J. M. (2003). *Getting Mentored in Graduate School..* Washington, DC: American Psychological Association.

Lumsden, D. B. (2000) *The Ph.D. Experience: Multidisciplinary Perspectives.* Brighton, NY: Accelerated Development.

Paredes, A. M. (2000). *Play The Game: How To Get Accepted and Succeed in Graduate School..* Phildelphia, PA: Xlibris Corporation.

Peters, R. L. (1997). *Getting What You Came for: The Smart Student's Guide to Earning a Master's or a Ph.D.* New York: Noonday Press.

Pittman, V. V. (1997). *Surviving Graduate School Part Time.* Thousand Oaks, CA: Sage Publications.

Walfish, S., & Hess, A. K. (Editors) (2001) *Succeeding in Graduate School: The Career Guide for Psychology Students.* Mahwah, NJ: Erlbaum.

WEB RESOURCES

Careers in Psychology

Considering Graduate School? Answer These Five Questions Before You Decide
http://www.quintcareers.com/considering_graduate_school.html

Primary Full-time Employment Settings of 1996 Masters Degree Recipients in Psychology
http://research.apa.org/mas4.html

Employment Settings of 1992 Baccalaureate Recipients in Psychology
http://research.apa.org/bac3.html
Where were 1992 Psychology Baccalaureate Recipients in 1994?
http://research.apa.org/bac8.html
Marky Lloyd's Careers in Psychology Page
http://www.psywww.com/careers/index.htm
Master's and Myth: Little Known Information About a Popular Degree
http://www.psichi.org/pubs/articles/article_90.asp
Interesting Careers in Psychology
http://www.apa.org/science/nonacad_careers.html
Fields of Psychology
http://www.psichi.org/content/publications/eye/category/fields.asp
Early Career Psychologists
http://www.apa.org/earlycareer/
Alternative Careers
http://www.apa.org/monitor/feb01/careerpath.html
Appreciating the PsyD: The Facts
http://www.psichi.org/pubs/articles/article_171.asp
Clinical Versus Counseling Psychology: What's the Diff?
http://www.psichi.org/pubs/articles/article_73.asp

Career Exploration

Career Assessment
http://www.quintcareers.com/career_assessment.html
Self-Directed Search
http://www.self-directed-search.com
Career Exploration
http://psychology.arizona.edu/resources/detail.php?option=8

Locating and Choosing Among Graduate Programs

Psychology Graduate Programs and Rankings
http://gradschool.about.com/cs/psychprograms/
Graduate School Directory
http://www.gradschools.com
Graduate School and Program Search
http://petersons.com/GradChannel/code/search.asp?
Research and Explore Schools on the Princeton Review
http://princetonreview.com/grad/research/
Choosing a Graduate Program
http://www.geocities.com/Heartland/Flats/5353/classes/how_to_decide_between.html

Preparing for Graduate School: Improving Your Credentials

Success in Fieldwork
    http://www.psichi.org/pubs/articles/article_40.asp
The Savvy Psychology Major
    http://www.psichi.org/pubs/articles/article_172.asp
Tips for Doing Well in Psychology Courses
    http://www.psichi.org/pubs/articles/article_13.asp
What Does Your Transcript Say About You, and What Can You Do If It Says Things
You Don't Like?
    http://www.psichi.org/pubs/articles/article_341.asp
Applications That Make the Schools You Want, Want You
    http://www.psichi.org/pubs/articles/article_124.asp
Does Research Experience Make a Significant Difference in Graduate Admissions?
    http://www.psichi.org/pubs/articles/article_67.asp
Finding Opportunities to Get Involved in Research: Some Advice From the Students'
Perspective
    http://www.psichi.org/pubs/articles/article_45.asp
Maximizing Undergraduate Opportunities: The Value of Research and Other Expe-
riences
    http://www.psichi.org/pubs/articles/article_39.asp
How to Prepare for Class
    http://www.towson.edu/~loiselle/rdingshelp.html
Participating in Class Discussions
    http://www.sas.upenn.edu/cwic/docs/ds2.doc

Overview of the Application Process

A Suggested Plan for Grad School Admission
    http://www.psynt.iupui.edu/undgrad/timeline.htm
Psychology Graduate Applicant's Portal
    http://www.psychgrad.org/
Advice for Undergraduates Considering Graduate School
    http://dlis.gseis.ucla.edu/people/pagre/grad-school.html
A Time Line for Applying to Graduate School
    http://www.psywww.com/careers/time-grd.htm
About Graduate School
    http://gradschool.about.com

Financial Aid: Paying for Graduate School

Student Eligibility for Federal Aid
    http://www.fafsa.ed.gov/before002.htm

FastWeb Scholarship Search
    http://www.fastweb.com
Scholarship Resource Network Express: Scholarship Search
    http://www.srnexpress.com/index.cfm
FinAid: Smart Student's Guide to Financial Aid
    http://www.finaid.org/
Student Guide to Financial Aid (US Govt. Publication)
    http://studentaid.ed.gov/students/publications/student_guide/index.html

The Graduate Record Exam

Peterson's Online Practice GRE Test and Scoring (for a fee)
    http://www.petersons.com/TestPrep/code/prompt.asp?sponsor=1&referer_type
    =CC&test_id=2
Princeton Review
    http://www.princetonreview.com
Kaplan
    http://www.kaptest.com
So You Wanna Ace the GRE
    http://www.soyouwanna.com/site/syws/acegre/acegre.html
So You Wanna Learn the Basics of the GRE
    http://www.soyouwanna.com/site/syws/basicgre/basicgre.html
Official GRE Site
    http://www.gre.org
Demystifying the GRE Psychology Test: A Brief Guide for Students
    http://www.psichi.org/pubs/articles/article_66.asp

Test Anxiety

Dealing with Test Anxiety
    http://www.petersons.com/testprepchannel/dealing_with_test_anxiety.asp
Test Anxiety
    http://www.uiowa.edu/web/advisingcenter/aac_curr_students/improving/test%
    20anxiety.htm
Stress Management Before the Test
    http://www.learnatest.com/generalinfo/testpreptips/stressbeforetest.cfm
Let Go of Test Anxiety
    http://www.sju.edu/lrc/print_examanxiety.htm

Personal Statements and Admissions Essays

Writing Personal Statements
    http://www.hope.edu/academic/psychology/geninfo/perstate.html

Writing the Graduate School Application Essay
    http://www.quintcareers.com/graduate_school.html
Essay Tips
    http://www.geocities.com/Heartland/Flats/5353/classes/purpose.html
Graduate School Statement
    http://career.berkeley.edu/Grad/GradStatement.stm
Personal Statements and Application Letters
    http://www.indiana.edu/~wts/wts/perstate.html
Writing a Compelling Personal Statement
    http://www.psichi.org/pubs/article.asp?article_id=98
The "Personal" Side of Graduate School Personal Statements
    http://www.psichi.org/pubs/article.asp?article_id=165

Writing a Curriculum Vitae

Writing a CV
    http://www.umt.edu/career/cv.htm
Preparing a Vitae
    http://www.quintcareers.com/curriculum_vitae.html
Writing a Vitae
    http://www.caps.mcgill.ca/static/student/workshops/cvwrite.html
Writing an Effective CV
    http://www.careers.ucr.edu/Students/Graduates/CV/
Writing Your CV
    http://gradschool.about.com/cs/curriculumvita/index.htm

Letters of Recommendation

What is a Recommendation Letter?
    http://www.a2zcolleges.com/adm/recinfo.htm
Getting a Good Letter of Recommendation
    http://www.psichi.org/pubs/articles/article_75.asp
It Takes More Than Good Grades! Some Straight Talk About How to Get Strong Letters of Recommendation From Faculty
    http://www.psichi.org/pubs/articles/article_135.asp
Asking for a Reference
    http://www.drlynnfriedman.com/psychologistreference.html
How to Get Good Letters of Recommendation
    http://www.psywww.com/careers/lettrec.htm
Advice on letters of recommendation
    http://www.socialpsychology.org/rectips.htm
Asking for a Recommendation
    http://www.jobsearch.bz/recommendations-2.php
Whom to ask and how
    http://www.career.cornell.edu/students/grad/health/HCEC/who.html

After Submitting the Application

Commando Tactics while Waiting
  http://dave.burrell.net/guide/guide5.html
Waiting for a Decision
  http://www.alumni.caltech.edu/~natalia/studyinus/guide/waiting.htm

Admissions Interviews

Tips for Your Graduate School Interview
  http://www.providence.edu/bio/grad/interviewP.pdf
Interviewing with Graduate or Professional Schools
  http://www.northwestern.edu/careers/STUDENTS/grad-prof/gradinterview
  .htm
Graduate School Interviewing Tips
  http://advisingservices.ucdavis.edu/pregrad/pdfs/grad_school_interview_tips
  .pdf
Handling Phone Interviews
  http://www.rcjobs.com/seeker-resources/phone_interview.html

Making Decisions

Deciding Among Offers
  http://career.ucsb.edu/students/applygradschl/deciding.html
Dealing with Rejection
  http://www.collegeconfidential.com/college_admissions/admission_rejection
  .htm

Transition to Graduate School

The Ideal Graduate Student
  http://wocket.csl.uiuc.edu/~loui/ideal.html
Congratulations! You've Been Accepted Into a Clinical Psychology Program! Now
What?
  http://www.psichi.org/pubs/articles/article_43.asp
Making the Transition to Graduate School
  http://www.psichi.org/pubs/articles/article_51.asp
Advice from Graduate Students About Making the Transition
  http://www-gse.berkeley.edu/program/sp/html/sptransition.html
Transition to Grad School
  http://gradschool.about.com/cs/transitions/

On Mentors and Advisors

Choosing a Mentor
    http://www.psichi.org/pubs/articles/article_107.asp
An Insider's Guide to Choosing a Graduate Adviser
    http://www.ou.edu/cas/botany-micro/grad-stu.html
How to Choose an Advisor
    http://www.cc.gatech.edu/faculty/ashwin/wisdom/how-to-choose-an-advisor
    .html
How to Deal with Faculty
    http://www.cc.gatech.edu/faculty/ashwin/wisdom/how-to-deal-with-faculty.html
Mentor and Graduate Student Strategies for Success
    http://graduate.louisville.edu/mentorhandbook.htm
How to Get the Mentoring You Want
    http://www.rackham.umich.edu/StudentInfo/Publications/StudentMentoring/
    contents.html
The Importance of Being Mentored
    http://www.psichi.org/pubs/articles/article_370.asp

Graduate School Survival and Success

Dealing with Procrastination
    http://gradschool.about.com/cs/procrastination/index.htm
Publishing: Advice and Information
    http://gradschool.about.com/cs/publishing/index.htm
So long, and thanks for the PhD!
    http://www.cs.unc.edu/~azuma/hitch4.html
Graduate School Survival Guide
    http://www-smi.stanford.edu/people/pratt/smi/advice.html
How to be a Good Graduate Student
    http://www.cs.indiana.edu/how.2b/how.2b.html
The Graduate School Years
    http://www.apa.org/students/student4.html
A Guide for Students in Professional Schools
    http://dlis.gseis.ucla.edu/people/pagre/leader.html
How to Succeed in Graduate School: A Guide for Students and Advisors
    http://info.acm.org/crossroads/xrds1-2/advice1.html
Student Stress: Effects and Solutions
    http://www.ericfacility.net/ericdigests/ed284514.html
Surviving Graduate School
    http://gradschool.about.com/cs/survival/
12 Tips for Surviving Graduate School
    http://www.cen-chemjobs.org/campus/cc_12tips.html

Time Management
    http://wonderland.hcii.cs.cmu.edu/Randy/timetalk.htm
What You Can Do as a Second Year Grad Student
    http://career.berkeley.edu/PhDs/PhD2ndyear.stm

REFERENCES

Actkinson, T. R. (2000). Master's and myth: Little-known information about a popular degree. *Eye on Psi Chi, 4*(2), 19–21, 23, 25.

American Association for Marriage and Family Therapy. (2002). *Directory of MFT licensing boards.* Retrieved on September 28, 2002 at http://www.aamft.org/resources/Online_Directories/boardcontacts.htm

American Occupational Therapy Association. (2002). *A career in occupational therapy: A rewarding choice in health care.* Retrieved on September 28, 2002 at http://www.aota.org/featured/area2/links/link09.asp

American Psychological Association. (1997). *Getting in: A step-by-step plan for gaining admission to graduate school in psychology.* Washington, DC: Author.

Appleby, D.C. (1990). *Graduate school superstars.* Retrieved on June 10, 2003 at http://www/psywww.com/careers/superstr.htm

Bonifazi, D. Z., Crespy, S. D., & Rieker, P. (1997). Value of a master's degree for gaining admission to doctoral programs in psychology. *Teaching of Psychology, 24,* 176–182.

Fisher, C. B., & Osofsky, J. (1997). Training the applied developmental scientist for prevention and practice: Two current examples, *Social Policy Report, 11*(2), 1–18.

Hays-Thomas, R. L. (2000). The silent conversation: Talking about the master's degree. *Professional Psychology: Research and Practice, 31,* 339–345.

Himelein, M. J. (1999). A student's guide to careers in the helping professions. *Office of Teaching Resources in Psychology.* Retrieved on January 3, 2001 at http://www.lemoyne.edu/OTRP/otrpresources/helping.html.

Keith-Spiegel, P., Tabachnick, B. G., & Spiegel, G. B. (1994). When demand exceeds supply: Second order criteria used by graduate school selection committees. *Teaching of Psychology, 21,* 79–81.

Keith-Spiegel, P., & Wiederman, M. W. (2000). *The complete guide to graduate school admission: Psychology, counseling, and related professions.* Mahwah, NJ: Erlbaum.

Kuther, T. L. (2003). *The psychology major's handbook.* Pacific Grove, CA: Wadsworth.

Kuther, T. L. (2004). *Your career in psychology: Psychology and law.* Pacific Grove, CA: Wadsworth.

Kuther, T. L., & Morgan, R. (2004). *Careers in psychology: Opportunities in a changing world.* Pacific Grove, CA: Wadsworth.

Landrum, E., Davis, S., & Landrum, T. (2000). *The psychology major: Career options and strategies for success.* Upper Saddle River, NJ: Prentice Hall.

National Center for Education Statistics. (2001). *Degrees and other awards conferred: 1999–2000.* Retrieved on January 25, 2002 from http://nces.ed.gov/pubs2002/2002156.pdf

Peters, R. L. (1992). *Getting what you came for: The smart student's guide to earning a master's or a PhD.* New York: Noonday Press.

University of Michigan. (2002). *How to get the mentoring you want.* Retrieved on June 10, 2003 at http://www.rackham.umich.edu/StudentInfo/Publications/Student-Mentoring/mentoring.pdf.

University of New Orleans. (2001). *Applied developmental psychology: Departmental program brochure.* Retrieved on July 2, 2002 at http://www.uno.edu/~psyc/adbroch2001.pdf

U.S. Bureau of Labor Statistics. (2002). *Occupational outlook handbook.* Washington, DC: Author.

INDEX

A

Acceptance, 70, 115, 118, 133–135
Accreditation, 33–34, 36
Actkinson, T. R., 3, 5, 6, 178
Admissions (*also see* application)
    and research experience, 52–55
    and waitlist, 135–136
    applied experience, 52–56
    choosing programs, 32–39
    criteria, 43–48
    essay (*see* personal statement)
    faculty decisions regarding, 46–47
    geographical limits, 39
    improving credentials for, 48–56
    keeping organized, 31–32, 41, 58, 63–64
    locating programs, 26–31
    statistics, 26, 43
    timetable, 64–70
    waiting process, 117
    when to contact the admissions office,
        115–117
Advisor, 17, 18, 19, 20, 41,147–154
American Association for Marriage and
    Family Therapy, 8, 179
American Occupational Therapy Associa-
    tion, 8, 179
American Psychological Association (APA),
    30, 33, 179
Appleby, D. C., 146, 179
Application
    and curriculum vitae, 60–63
    and getting organized, 31–32, 41
    and transcripts, 59–60
    forms, 57–58, 68
    what to expect after submission, 114–115
Applied Experience, 4,6, 7, 8, 9–10, 13, 14,
    55–56, 65, 67, 91–92

Attrition, 37
Autobiographical essay, 91–92 (*also see* per-
    sonal statement)

B

Bachelor's degree, 3
Bonifazi, D. Z., 47, 179

C

Campus visit (*also see* interview), 40, 66–77
Careers
    with a doctoral degree, 11–17
    with a master's degree, 5–9
Certification, 6, 7, 8
Choosing (*see* deciding)
Comprehensive examinations, 4, 10, 17, 20
Counseling, 5, 7
Coursework
    graduate level, 18, 141–143
    preferred for graduate admission, 49–50
    retaking, 51, 67
Credentials
    for admission, 43–48
    improving, 48–56
Crespi, S. D., 47, 179
Curriculum vitae, 60–63, 67, 74–75
CV (*see* curriculum vitae)

D

Davis, S., 110, 179
Decisions
    about graduate study, 21–23, 28–29
    among programs, 32–39, 133–134
Declining an offer of admission, 134–135
Dissertation, 10, 11, 18, 20

Doctor of philosophy (*see* PhD)
Doctor of psychology (*see* PsyD)
Doctoral degree
    in developmental psychology, 16–17
    in experimental psychology, 15
    in health psychology, 13–14
    in industrial/organizational psychology,
        27
    in neuropsychology, 15
    in physiological psychology, 14
    in psychophysics, 15–16
    in quantitative psychology, 15–16
    in social psychology, 17
    in sport psychology, 13–14
    reasons for pursing, 9–10
    what does it entail, 9–10
    PhD verses PsyD, 10–11
    in clinical psychology, 10–12, 13, 27, 33
    in counseling psychology, 10–11, 12, 13,
        27, 33
    time to completion, 20, 21, 37
    in forensic psychology, 12–13

E

Email
    and admissions, 40–41
    etiquette, 40–41

F

Faculty (*also see* advisor, mentor)
    adjunct professor, 103
    assistant professor, 104
    associate professor, 104
    choosing among, 35–36
    contacting, 40–42, 115–117
    establishing relationships with, 64–65, 66,
        108–109, 144–145, 150–154
    professor, 104
Financial aid, 38, 68, 70–72
Fisher, C. B., 16, 178

G

Grade point average (GPA), 30, 31, 43,
    44–45, 46, 48–49, 50–51, 59, 64, 77
Graduate Admissions Examination (*see*
    GRE)

Graduate school
    admission (*see* Admissions)
    advantages, 20
    and prestige, 38–39
    as apprenticeship, 18–19
    classes, 18, 141–143
    disadvantages, 21
    is it for you?, 21–23
    moving to attend, 39
    research, 18–19, 144, 159–160
    success, 18, 22, 43–44, 46–47, 146–147
    transition, 154–163
    what it is like, 17–21, 141–146
    working before attending, 23–24
Graduate student
    average age, 24
    tips, 42, 56, 75–76, 88, 99–100, 112–113,
        130–132, 139–140, 162–163
Graduate study (*see* graduate school)
GRE, 24, 30, 31, 35, 43, 44–45, 46, 59, 66,
    67, 68, 69, 115, 136, 138, 140
    analytical writing section, 81–82
    and test anxiety, 86–87
General Test, 59, 77–85
    preparation, 83–84
    quantitative section, 80–81
    registration, 78–79
    retaking the, 84–85
    scoring, 82
    Subject Test in Psychology, 59, 66,
        85–86
    verbal section, 79–80

H

Hays-Thomas, R. L., 4, 179
Himelein, M. J., 5, 6, 179

I

Internship, 4, 6, 7, 8, 9, 13, 14
Interview, 70, 115, 120–132
    and anxiety, 128–129
    common questions, 123–125
    preparing for, 121–122
    purpose of, 120–121
    tips, 127–128
    what to ask, 125–127
    what to expect, 121, 122–123

K

Keith-Spiegel, P., 43, 46, 47, 90, 116, 178
Kuther, T. L., 4, 5, 6, 9, 13, 15, 16, 17, 22, 27, 92, 138, 179

L

Landrum, E., 110, 179
Landrum, T., 110, 179
Letters of recommendation, 24, 44, 45, 60, 67, 68, 69, 101–113, 115, 136
Licensure, 5, 6, 8, 10

M

Marriage and family therapy, 5, 8
Master's degree
    and independent practice, 5, 6, 7
    in clinical psychology, 4, 5
    in counseling, 7
    in counseling psychology, 4, 5
    in industrial/organizational psychology, 6
    in marriage and family therapy, 8
    in occupational therapy, 7–8
    in psychology, 4, 5
    in research areas of psychology, 9
    in school psychology, 4, 5–6
    in social work, 6
    in speech language pathology, 8–9
    M.A. verses M. S., 4
    number awarded, 3, 4
    process, 4, 17
    reasons for pursing, 4
    thesis, 4, 17
Mentor, 10, 47–154
Morgan, R. D., 4, 5, 6, 9, 13, 15, 16, 17, 28, 92, 179

N

National Board of Certified Counselors and Affiliates, 7
National Center for Education Statistics, 3, 180
Networking, 31, 399, 144–145

O

Occupational therapy, 7–8

Online admissions forms, 57–58
Osofsky, J., 16, 179

P

Personal statement, 44, 45–46, 58–59, 67, 69, 89–98, 115
    and writer's block, 94–95
    common topics, 90–92
    revising the, 95–96
Peters, R., 38, 180
PhD, 10, 13, 18, 20, 52, 55
Practicum (see applied experience)
Professional psychologist-practitioner model, 28
Psychology and the law (see forensic psychology)
Psychology major, 49
PsyD, 11, 28

R

Recommendation letters (*see* letters of recommendation)
Rejection, 70, 115, 118, 136–139
Research
    and personal statement, 91–92
    assistant, 54–55, 109–111
    assistantship, 73
    experience, 24, 109–111
    how to get involved in, 52–53, 65, 109
    journal, 159–160
    why do it, 53–54
Research-scientist model, 27

S

School psychologist, 5–6
Scientist-practitioner model, 27
Self assessment
    choosing programs, 32–39
    personal statement, 93–94, 98–99
Specialist's degree, 6
Speech pathology, 8–9
Statement of purpose (*see* personal statement)
Stress management, 128–129, 160–162
Study tips, 50–51, 155–159
Supervised experience (*see* internship, applied experience)

T

Tabachnick, B. G., 47, 43
Teaching
    assistant, 10, 20
    assistantship, 72–73
Test anxiety, 86–87
Thesis, 17, 20
Time off before graduate school, 23–25
Tips from graduate students, 42, 56, 75–76,
        88, 99–100, 112–113, 130–132,
        139–140, 162–163

Training models, 27–28
Transcript, 59–60, 67, 68, 69, 106, 115
Transition to graduate school, 154–163

W

Wait-list, 135–136
Wiederman, M. W., 46, 90, 116
Work experience, 24